Pantheon

The Welsh

What People Are Saying About

Pantheon: The Welsh

Distilling a wide array of material into a single, easy to understand text, *Pantheon: the Welsh* is a must read for anyone interested in Welsh paganism or beliefs. This book offers insight into everything from magic to myths and from Gods to holidays, with plenty of practical tips and exercises mixed in. Perfect for the beginner and great to have on hand as a reference.
Morgan Daimler, author of *Gods and Goddesses of Ireland* and *Pantheon: The Irish*

An Insightful and engaging book that would make the Bards of old sing their praises, Mhara provides a rich corpus of knowledge to illuminate the sacred cosmology of Wales. With accurately sourced information and accessible elements to incorporate into magical practice, *Pantheon: The Welsh* is the perfect book for all seeking connection to the Deities of this enchanting landscape.
Brett Hollyhead, author of *Sabrina: Discovering the Goddess of the River Severn*

Pantheon

The Welsh

Mhara Starling

London, UK
Washington, DC, USA

First published by Moon Books, 2026
Moon Books is an imprint of Collective Ink Ltd.,
Unit 11, Shepperton House, 89 Shepperton Road, London, N1 3DF
office@collectiveinkbooks.com
www.collectiveinkbooks.com
www.moon-books.net

For distributor details and how to order please visit the 'Ordering' section on our website.

ISBN: 978 1 80341 742 4
978 1 80341 741 7 (ebook)
Library of Congress Control Number: 2025933260

A CIP catalogue record for this book is available from the British Library.

Design: Lapiz Digital Services
Cover Artwork: The Tarot for the Sidhe. Dreamer 3 Card. Emily Carding. 2010. Schiffer.

UK: Printed and bound by CPI Group (UK) Ltd, Croydon, CR0 4YY
US: Printed and bound by Thomson-Shore, 7300 West Joy Road, Dexter, MI 48130

The manufacturer's authorised representative in the EU for product safety is:
eucomply OÜ - Pärnu mnt 139b-14, 11317 Tallinn, Estonia, hello@ eucompliancepartner.com,
www.eucompliancepartner.com

Contents

Introduction 1

Part I

Chapter 1 – History 7
Chapter 2 – Mythology 11
Chapter 3 – Cosmology 31
Chapter 4 – Magic 42
Chapter 5 – Apotheosis 51
Chapter 6 – Seasonal Celebrations 58
Chapter 7 – Putting It into Practice 70

Part II

Chapter 8 – Deities 77
Chapter 9 – Spirits Seen and Unseen 130

Conclusion 135
A Guide to Welsh Pronunciation 137
Bibliography 142

This Book is Dedicated to the Anglesey Druid Order.
Thank you for offering me a sense of belonging,
a community, a spiritual home.

Introduction

Long before I ever referred to myself as a Pagan, a Polytheist, an Animist, or a Witch, I believed that the landscape around me was alive and teeming with spirits. I was not raised in any particular religion, and so, beyond the odd mention of Biblical stories at school, or being cast in the nativity play around Christmas, no God played much of a role in my upbringing. Despite this, I knew in my heart that there was something divine out there, reaching out to us.

I grew up in a small village with a population of only around five hundred people. A coastal village located in the South-West of *Ynys Môn*, the Isle of Anglesey, in North Wales. Despite how tiny the village is, we had numerous churches and chapels dotted around the place. However, the place I considered most sacred in the village, was a cliff overlooking the sea. On the coastal path, just where the river Ffraw bent around and joined with the sea, was a headland covered in lush green grass. A stone bench overlooked the black coastal rocks, beaches, and the waves below. But just at the edge of the headland, before the cliff led down to the water, was a strange scattering of stones.

Organised in the shape of a crescent moon, an almost full circle of stones that came up to around my knees. I always felt drawn to these stones, as though they were vibrating, pulling me in to whisper secret things in my ears. There, in this place where the land, sky, and sea sang together in perfect harmony, I felt the divine. To me, the divine was not found in a church, or in the pages of a big old book. They were singing upon the winds, humming with the endless sky above, pulsating with the telluric power of the dirt and stone beneath my feet, and dancing in the waves.

It was years later, after I had discovered the path of modern Paganism and Witchcraft that I learnt that this place, those stones I so loved, were the remnants of an ancient monument. A cairn dating back to the Bronze Age. It filled me with such glee to discover that archaeologists had excavated this space long before I was born, and they had found evidence of ritual activity. It was a place where the dead was laid to rest, where hazelnuts were burnt, and flint blades were piled up in the centre of what was once a ring of stone. I had no idea just how much history rested beneath my feet when I visited this space multiple times a week as a teenager. I truly believe something was reaching out to me, calling me to wake up and familiarise myself with the ancient currents of the land I called home. And I'm certain many of you have felt that same call, hence why you have picked up this book.

When I first began dipping my toes into the realms of modern-day Paganism and Polytheism, I, like many others, looked to well-known and beloved Gods from landscapes far, far away. One of my first pieces of Pagan jewellery was a pentagram held up by a silver figure of the Egyptian Goddess, Isis. I had a love for the Greek God, Poseidon, due to my affinity for the sea and the fact I lived on the coast. It was not until I was a little older that I began wondering *what about the Gods of here? Of this place? Those whose stories are immersed in the landscape I interact with daily?*

With that question in mind I met with Kristoffer Hughes, head of the Anglesey Druid Order. He introduced me to the Gods he and the Druid Order worked with. I was shocked to realise I already knew these Gods. Arianrhod, Brân, Rhiannon, Gwydion to name a few...these were all familiar names. Having been raised speaking Welsh as my native language and attending a school which taught all its classes via the medium of the Welsh language, I was intimately familiar with the stories of the *Mabinogi*. It was not until I found my way into Paganism, however, that I began to think of the characters in such stories as Gods.

Within the pages of this book, I would like to take you on a journey to meet the Deities of Wales. Via history, mythology, literature, folklore, language, and magic we will delve into the very pantheon of Gods that have emerged from the landscape that is Cymru.

Part I of this book provides the theoretical background behind the topic of Welsh Deities. We will explore the history of Wales, the myths that are part and package of our culture, and touch upon topics such as *are the Welsh Gods really Gods?*

The second part of this book will act as an index to several of our Gods, Goddesses, divinities, and spirits. Providing you with enough information to hopefully springboard you into constructing a meaningful relationship with them.

Part I

Chapter 1

History

In this rugged, ancient landscape of mountain and coast, valley and stream, river and hill, are the stories of a time when the roars of dragons echoed through the stormy skies. Tales of wizards with the ability to transform the shape of one being into another, and of giants who ruled the land with compassion and strength. This is Cymru.

Before we drink from the cauldron of myth and legend in order to part the mists on the Deities of our culture and landscape, it would be beneficial for us to learn a little of the history of Wales and her people. Our mythology and magic are linked deeply with our language, landscape, and culture. This will not be by any means an exhaustive look into the history of our nation, but I hope I am able to capture a little of our spirit so that the lore you will learn of throughout this book can be rooted in its cultural context.

Who Are the Cymry?

Located to the Western region of what is today referred to as the United Kingdom, Wales is a nation with its own distinct culture, language, and identity. Long living in the shadow of our neighbours to the East, the English, our culture has faced many hardships and battles for the right to exist. However, regardless of such hardships, we stand strong. As the famous words of Dafydd Iwan's moving song utters: *Er gwaetha pawb a phopeth, ry'n ni yma o hyd!* In spite of everyone and everything, we are still here!

The Welsh language developed from the ancient common Brittonic language, and indeed is the oldest language spoken in Britain today (Davies, 1999). Due to centuries of suppression of the language and our culture many people in Wales today do not speak our language. And yet, it is important to acknowledge that it is not a 'dead' language, nor has it ever truly even been a 'dying' language. When we look at our nation and explore the number of Welsh speakers on a statistical level, Welsh clearly appears as a minority language. And yet, countless communities across Wales, including the one I grew up in, speak Welsh as their primary mode of communication. In these areas the language is a majority language, and you will hardly ever hear English spoken. Indeed, I never spoke English with any regularity until I left secondary school (high school) and ventured to college. This is the experience of many people who grew up in Welsh speaking areas across Wales.

It is important to acknowledge as well that Wales is classed as its own country. The notion that we are a 'principality' is a common misconception or misunderstanding. On all official levels Wales is recognised as a country. To say that Wales is not a country is to essentially say that England or Scotland are not countries.

Whilst the title of this book features the word 'Welsh', it is important to acknowledge the native name for our country and what it is we call ourselves. Whilst I do refer to myself as Welsh within Anglo-centric settings for ease and comfort, in my first language I refer to myself as a *Cymraes*. This word describes a woman who is Welsh. The native name for the country itself is *Cymru* and when we spell it *Cymry* it refers to the people of our nation. The masculine equivalent to the term I call myself would be *Cymro*.

Here is a handy chart to illustrate the native words we have to describe our nation, language, and people.

Wales (The Country)	Cymru
The Welsh People	Cymry
The Welsh Language	Cymraeg
A Welsh Woman	Cymraes
A Welsh Man	Cymro

The Celtic Conundrum

Our language is part of a family tree known as the 'Celtic languages'. We are related most closely to languages such as Cornish, and Breton. However, we are also related to Scottish Gaelic, Irish, and Manx.

All of these languages mentioned above, and many others, fall under the umbrella term of being 'Celtic Languages'. However, they fall into two distinct family groups. There are the Q-Celtic or Goidelic languages of Irish, Manx, and Scottish Gaelic. And then there are the P-Celtic or Brythonic languages of Welsh, Cornish, and Breton. This is not an exhaustive list and explanation of all the Celtic languages, but rather a snapshot of the complexity of the umbrella term 'Celtic' within the context of language.

All of these languages are Celtic, but not all are Gaelic. A common misconception I see is the idea that the Welsh language is a 'Gaelic' language, with some people even referring to it as 'Welsh Gaelic'. Cymraeg is not a Gaelic language, and simply referring to it as 'Welsh' or 'Cymraeg' is most accurate.

Because of the fact that our language is indeed part of the Celtic family of languages, our culture is also identified by many as being Celtic in nature. Beyond this we are also classed as a modern-day Celtic nation. However, it is important to acknowledge that the word 'Celtic' can nowadays be considered rather controversial.

Within modern scholarship there are numerous debates as to whether the term 'Celtic' means anything at all outside of the context of language. And indeed, beyond this, the term has long been romanticised (Green & Howell, 2000).

One of the biggest issues which arises out of the 'Celtic debate' is the notion that being 'Celtic' is somehow related to DNA, blood, or ancestry. This idea is incredibly popular outside of the modern-day Celtic nations and can often lead to rather ridiculous, and even dangerous ideas of who can or cannot claim a Celtic identity.

At its root the term Celtic is used primarily to denote cultural markers. Language is the primary marker, but we might also look to things such as art, food, stories. All of these things are related to culture, not DNA or blood.

Culture Is Lived

Culture is not something that we are necessarily naturally born to. Our culture is influenced by the language we speak, the foods we eat, the songs we sing, the stories we tell. None of this is determined entirely by our race, our genetics, or indeed even necessarily always our ancestry. Of course, ancestry might play a role in our cultural understanding of the world, but it is not the only thing that links us to culture.

Culture is lived. It is expressed daily and colours our worldview and day-to-day experiences. I am not Welsh because my ancestry hails from Wales, or my blood is of this soil. I am Welsh because the Welsh language is my mother tongue, the hills and mountains of this country were the backdrop to my childhood, the traditional foods I ate growing up, the dances I learnt, the culture I was immersed in were all Welsh.

Chapter 2

Mythology

The most obvious place to start when searching for information regarding the Welsh Deities is, of course, mythology. Our stories sing the songs of the landscape, granting us a glimpse into a mythic view of our people, spirits, Deities, and lore. However, it can be somewhat daunting and a tad confusing to approach the myths at first. Where does one even begin?

The lore pertaining to Welsh Deities can be found across numerous sources – from prose tales preserved in medieval manuscripts, to epic poems, and even in folk tales and folk customs. In this chapter I have outlined the primary places to turn to when seeking information pertaining to the entities we might choose to revere and work with within our practices today. Here you will find a bit of information regarding what these sources are, how to navigate them, which versions to pick up today, and the history of their translations and such to this day.

Whilst it is perfectly fine to simply dive into these various sources without any prior knowledge of their histories and cultural context, I believe that by having a better understanding of what exactly it is you are diving into, you will be able to approach the myths, poems, and stories with greater ease. My advice is to read through this chapter and then to begin your search for modern editions and translations of the texts mentioned. They will all grant you a much greater understanding of the Deities we will be exploring later in this book.

The Four Branches of the *Mabinogi*

Of all the various streams one might glean information regarding the magic, mystery, and divinities of the Welsh landscape, the

Four Branches of the *Mabinogi* are likely the most well-known. The stories that comprise the Four Branches have been translated into English and many other languages by today, and you can easily pick up a copy from your local bookseller. Due to this accessibility, and the fact the stories are deeply enigmatic and gripping, the Four Branches have inspired lovers of mythology, fantasy fiction authors, poets, artists, and even modern-day streams of Paganism and Witchcraft for years upon years.

What we refer to as the Four Branches of the *Mabinogi* are a collection of Welsh prose tales which were preserved in medieval manuscripts. It has long been debated how old exactly the manuscripts themselves are (Charles-Edwards, 1996). Scholars of the past, such as Sir Ifor Williams were of the opinion that the written versions of the stories as we know them today were written down during the 11th century. More recent scholarship, however, prefers to date them to a later time in the medieval period.

The stories themselves, however, hold echoes of an older tradition of oral storytelling (Davies, 2007). What this means is that the written versions of the stories are not necessarily the oldest versions. In fact, it is believed that the stories as they are recorded in medieval manuscripts such as the *Red Book of Hergest* and the *White Book of Rhydderch* are essentially copies of copies. We can never know for certain how old exactly the stories themselves are, nor how much they might have changed over time before eventually being preserved onto ink and paper. However, it is clear that during the medieval period, a tumultuous period for the Welsh who were fighting to preserve their heritage and culture amidst constant invasions and attacks, nobles who had the resources to do so clearly viewed these stories as worthy of being remembered.

Long before the words were put to paper, however, it is likely that these stories were living, breathing things. Not only told but performed by a learned *Cyfarwydd*, a traditional storyteller, around campfires, in the courts of castles, and at important community events.

Themes, characters, and ideas woven throughout the Four Branches are today easily recognisable to many with an interest in Celtic mythology. It is in this tradition of storytelling we find the stories of Rhiannon, Branwen, Brân the Blessed, Arianrhod, Lleu Llaw Gyffes, Gwydion and many other characters who are now revered across the world as Gods by modern day Polytheists, Pagans, and Witches.

But why do we call them the Four Branches? In Welsh the stories are referred to as *Pedair Cainc Y Mabinogi,* literally 'the Four Branches of the *Mabinogi*'. Naming the stories as branches leads us to envision them in our minds as a body of lore connected to one mighty tree, with each story acting as a branch jutting out from the main tree trunk. This is a beautiful, poetic, and useful visualisation of the stories. They grow, twisted and gnarled, winding around one another, branching off into smaller twigs that lead down strange yet entertaining tangents.

The idea of the stories being referred to as branches comes from the manuscripts within which they are preserved. At the end of certain story cycles the text reads:

> *Ac Felly Terfyna'r Gainc Hon o'r Mabinogi*
> (And thus ends this branch of the *Mabinogi*)

This indicates to us that the primary storyline or cycle we were previously following has come to an end, and now we are embarking on a new venture. However, it must be remembered that the stories themselves are intimately connected with one another as well, made abundantly clear by recurring characters, storylines which act as the direct consequences of events which unfolded in previous branches, references to certain events and ideas mentioned earlier etc.

This system gives the Four Branches a sense of seriality and continuation. We are being immersed in a world and a story which might at times feel disjointed and confusing, yet we are constantly reminded that each story, at its core, connects to the same root, the same tree. Move over Marvel Cinematic Universe, the *Mabinogi* did it first!

The stories which make up the Four Branches are:

1. Pwyll Pendefig Dyfed (Pwyll, Prince of Dyfed)
2. Branwen ferch Llŷr (Branwen, Daughter of Llŷr)
3. Manawydan fab Llŷr (Manawydan, Son of Llŷr)
4. Math fab Mathonwy (Math, Son of Mathonwy)

And whilst these stories are saturated with concepts of magic, Otherworldly contact, shapeshifting, giants, magical cauldrons, and seemingly divine beings, they are at their heart also grounded stories about family, shame and reparation, morality, and leadership. It is this mixture of the fantastical and the mundane which I believe make the stories so deeply relatable, enthralling, and entertaining. Despite having been put to pen and paper in the medieval period, these stories could easily rival the likes of Tolkien's stories, or *Game of Thrones* today. And, in fact, these popular pieces of fantasy literature draw a lot of inspiration from the Four Branches of the *Mabinogi*.

To learn more about the Four Branches, I recently wrote another book on this subject alone as part of the *Pagan Portals* series. Do search for that book in order to delve deeper into the *Mabinogi's* lore, magic, Deities, and history.

Beyond the Four Branches

If you are already acquainted with the *Mabinogi*, then you may be asking yourself at this moment: *'Wait, I have a copy of the Mabinogi…but my copy is called the Mabinogion, and definitely has more than four stories in it! What's going on?!'*. So, what exactly is the difference between the *Mabinogi* and the *Mabinogion*? Is there a difference at all? And what are these other stories that are usually included in translations today if they are *not* part of the corpus which makes up the Four Branches?

The Four Branches of the *Mabinogi* are referred to as such because of that line mentioned earlier at the end of each story cycle. However, there are other stories also found in the same manuscript tradition which do not end with such a line. These stories are not part of what might be considered the *Mabinogi* proper. The term *Mabinogi* only truly applies to the Four Branches (Davies, 1989). However, the other stories found in the same medieval manuscripts are often grouped together with the Four Branches as they are an expression of the same Welsh storytelling tradition.

When the Welsh texts were initially being translated into English by scholars such as William Owen Pughe and Lady Charlotte Guest in the 19th century, the word *Mabinogion* was believed to be a plural term used to describe any and all 'Juvenile Romances' (Bromwich, 1996). The word *Mabinogion* as opposed to *Mabinogi* appears at the end of the first branch and is by today believed to have likely been a scribal error (Ifans & Ifans, 2007).

Due to the word *Mabinogion* being used as a catch-all term by the early scholars for all the medieval prose texts preserved in manuscripts, however, the term stuck. Nowadays *Mabinogion* is likely more recognisable than the arguably more correct form *Mabinogi* outside of Wales. Academics to this day have adopted the term to describe the Four Branches of the *Mabinogi* and the further prose tales from the same Welsh tradition as a collection.

The stories you will likely see grouped together alongside the Four Branches in translations easily acquired today are:

- Breuddwyd Macsen Wledig (The Dream of Maxen Wledig)

- Lludd a Llefelys (Lludd and Llefelys)
- Culhwch ac Olwen (Culhwch and Olwen)
- Breuddwyd Rhonabwy (The Dream of Rhonabwy)
- Iarlles y Ffynnon / Owain (The Lady of the Fountain / Owain)
- Peredur fab Efrog (Peredur, son of York)
- Geraint fab Erbin (Geraint, son of Erbin)

These stories do not necessarily follow in any seriality to the Four Branches, but as they are preserved in the same manuscript tradition and rooted in a Welsh storytelling tradition it simply makes sense to include them alongside the Four Branches.

The tales beyond the Four Branches include the escapades of King Arthur and his court, epic romances incredibly comparable to the French literary romances, and stories with themes of prophecy and destiny. Beyond King Arthur other recognisable names found in these tales include Gwyn ap Nudd, Mabon son of Modron, and Elen Luyddog.

Beyond these stories there is also the story of the birth of Taliesin. In Lady Charlotte Guest's translation of Welsh prose texts, she included the tale of Cerridwen, a Witch who brews a potion to aid her hideously ugly son, but the potion is instead drunk by another boy who becomes the legendary Taliesin, the greatest bard and prophet in all Welsh lore. However, many modern translations will not include this story, and there is a reason for that.

Whilst the Four Branches and the further seven stories mentioned above are found in medieval manuscripts, the tale of Taliesin's birth, titled *Ystoria Taliesin,* is not. This story instead comes to us from an early modern manuscript dated to circa 1552 known as Elis Gruffudd's Chronicle. This places the story instead into the realms of later folklore as opposed to being part of the earlier storytelling tradition. However, it is worth noting that certain early Welsh poetry makes reference to the story of Taliesin's birth, indicating that whilst this 16th century version of the tale is the earliest literary version we know of, the story itself was likely known to those in Wales at the very least centuries prior.

The Triads

Beyond the prose tales preserved in medieval manuscripts, we may also glean some information regarding mythical, legendary, or heroic cultural characters and Deities from what is referred to as *Trioedd Ynys Prydein,* The Triads of the Island of Britain.

The Triads act as a catalogue, listing the various names of important cultural figures from the history, mythology, and legends of Britain. The Bards of Britain would have turned to this catalogue and used it as a sort of index which reminded them of the epic stories behind the rousing characters and figures who featured in the stories, poems, and songs of the past.

It is not merely the names of important cultural figures that are expressed in these triple groups known as the Triads. Along with names we also find facts and precepts. Some of the Triads list legendary battles, the courts of King Arthur, festivals, the names of horses, and disasters to name a few.

The names, concepts, legendary events and such are grouped together under specific epithets or descriptors. An example of a Triad would be:

Tri Bardd Kaw oedd yn Llys Arthur
Myrddin vab Morvryn,
Myrddyn Embrys,
A Thaliesin
Three Skilful Bards were at Arthur's Court
Myrddin, son of Morfryn,
Myrddin Emrys,
And Taliesin
(Bromwich, 2014)

In this Triad three skilled, or harmonious Bards which were under the patronage of the legendary King Arthur are listed. These three include two different epithets or names for Myrddin, the earlier Welsh equivalent to the infamous Arthurian wizard, Merlin. His two names here are Myrddin, son of Morfryn, who is referred to in other texts as Merlin Celidonius, and Myrddin Emrys, also known as Merlin Ambrosius. Alongside both epithets of Merlin or Myrddin we have the legendary Bard and prophet Taliesin.

What this Triad does, as they all do, is offer us a window into the lore and legend behind such characters in very few words. Those who knew the legends and stories of this landscape would have been able to read such a thing and then draw upon such themes to weave into their poetry, songs, and prophecies.

Many of the stories and themes mentioned in the Triads are from aspects of lore and legend which has now been long lost to us. They tell of stories such as the imprisonment of the mighty Llŷr, or they tell us that well known characters from the *Mabinogi,* such as Brân and Aranrhod, have children that are not featured in their most well-known myths. This grants us the knowledge that there were likely more stories and legends being shared once upon a time, stories which were performed, sung, and told by storytellers and Bards.

What the Triads can offer us, as modern-day Polytheists, Pagans, and Witches who draw upon the wellspring of Welsh tradition, is further information regarding the Deities and spiritual allies we work with and revere.

For example, Aranrhod (or sometimes better known as Arianrhod) appears in the fourth branch of the *Mabinogi.* We may glean information about the nature of Aranrhod from her name, which may indeed translate to mean something akin to 'The still point at the centre of the turning wheel'. In the fourth branch of the *Mabinogi,* she appears as the daughter of the Goddess Dôn, and a sister to the troublesome magician Gwydion. Aranrhod could be perceived as somewhat cold, unfeeling, and harsh in this branch. She enacts various *Tyngedau* (fates) upon her son which hinder him from being able to fully integrate into society. She is humiliated in the fourth branch, and in response she is rightfully angry. Aranrhod appears to reject motherhood, and as such rejects many of the socially expected roles placed upon her due to her gender. Another way one might interpret her based on this story is as a form of initiatrix. Perhaps her acts towards her son are not purely malicious, and they are the challenges he must face so that he grows into the warrior and leader he is destined to be.

Either way, the Aranrhod of the fourth branch of the *Mabinogi* is a transgressive, powerful, and complex Goddess. However, her lore is limited here. We have one story, one situation to learn about her within the context of. The Triads offer us a little more.

In Triad number 36, Aranrhod is described as the daughter of Beli, and she has two sons which are not mentioned in the *Mabinogi*. These sons are Gwanar and Gwennwynwyn. Aranrhod here, rather than being the independent woman tied to no man that she is in the *Mabinogi*, is instead a consort of Lliaws son of Nwyfre. The two sons mentioned above are the children of Aranrhod and Lliaws. This becomes increasingly more interesting as we translate the names of these entities. Her consort is Lliaws son of Nwyfre, which could be translated to mean 'Host, multitude son of the firmament'. Her sons are Gwennwynwyn – blessed or shining bright poison, and Gwanar – warrior lord.

The wheel's axle, the still point which enables the wheel to turn, is the consort of the multitude son of the skies or atmosphere. Together they bore the blessed, shining poison and a warrior ruler. This is a rather poetic interpretation of what is at play in this Triad, when delving into the etymology of the names. A poetic interpretation which we could explore on a spiritual or polytheistic level, gleaned from information provided within the Triads.

Triad 78 then refers to Aranrhod as one of the three fair and royal ladies of the island of Britain, alongside Creirwy, daughter of Cerridwen, and Gwen, daughter of Cywryd son of Crydon.

By looking at Aranrhod within the context of the *Mabinogi* and the Triads together, it paints a picture of a far more complex Goddess and more entities which she is connected to. This provides us with more to work with, a greater scope for approaching Aranrhod, and a better chance to fully understand her on a far more visceral level.

This could be said for many of the Deities of the Welsh tradition. Brân, Elen, Llŷr, Gwydion, Mabon and more appear in the Triads. Beyond the well-known characters featured in the *Mabinogi* and other prose tales, there are also mentions of more obscure, shadowy characters. There are no prose stories that are still known to us in the literary record relating to entities such as Llŷr, Don, and Beli who are mentioned only as parents or ancestors in the *Mabinogi*. However, in the Triads we find hints that narratives surrounding these ancient ancestors were likely known to the Bards of the past, and what little is preserved in the Triads offers us an opportunity to peer at a small part of said narratives.

Whilst the Triads do not offer us information that is fed in a digestible, linear, narrative pattern, the information is still incredibly valuable. I often view the Deities of Wales as complex jigsaw puzzles in many ways. In order to gain a clear, precise picture of who they are, we must find all the scattered pieces found in the myths, the poems, the Triads, the etymologies of their names, their links to other characters, and even sometimes elements of belief and lore found in folk traditions. Pulling these pieces together offers us a fuller picture of who they are and how we might approach them today.

Poetry

The Welsh are a nation of poets, and of singers. We sing this fact in our national anthem. Poetry has long been at the core of our cultural expression and continues to play a prominent role in who we are to this day.

The *National Eisteddfod* is an annual festival in Wales which celebrates poetry, music, and the arts via competitions and performances. A festival held over several days where the best of the best come to compete for their chance to be honoured. To win a chair or a crown at the Eisteddfod is a great honour indeed, and I would argue that it is in many ways the greatest of honours among Welsh speaking communities. Can you imagine? A nation where we celebrate the accomplishments of poets, singers, dancers, artists over those who fight in wars, politicians, or those who hoard the most money? There is something both humble and awe inspiring about that.

Whilst the Eisteddfod in its modern form was conceived primarily in the late eighteenth and through to the nineteenth centuries, there is evidence of similar contests and celebrations of poetry taking place throughout Welsh history. The bards of early Wales competed for the patronage of great rulers (Haycock, 2007). They had the ear of royalty, if they could demonstrate their remarkable skills in the art.

The poetry of Wales is another treasure trove where we can glean more information regarding the myth, magic, lore, and Deities of the landscape.

Welsh poetry as we know it today extends as far back as the sixth century. What might come as a surprise is that the oldest Welsh poetry that we have written record of does not come from the land we refer to as 'Wales' today. No, the oldest recorded Welsh poems were composed and written in what we would today refer to as the Northernmost regions of England and Southernmost regions of Scotland.

The poems from this era were composed in a time of unrest. Directly following the withdrawal of the Romans from Britain, and in a time where the old Saints walked the earth, the Anglo-Saxons were invading, and the native Britons were at each other's throats as a great power vacuum and cultural identity crisis took hold upon these islands. One of the oldest poems we have in the written record is known today as *Y Gododdin,* this poem sings the elegies of fallen warriors from the ancient Brythonic kingdom of the same name.

We could in many ways consider poetry a magical art within a Welsh cultural context. The bards, those who composed and sang the greatest of poems had the ear of royalty. Kings and leaders acted as patrons for the bards, for they knew that a bard had the ability to sing their praises and sway the people's perception of their rule.

Tony Conran, in his book *Welsh Verse,* discusses how the tradition of Welsh poetry has its roots in a form of ceremonial magic in which poems were uttered as invocations during rituals involving the funerals of great rulers, or the coronation of a new ruler (Conran, 2017). The bards within this context were essentially magicians, responsible for holding important ritualistic ceremonies which would change the cultural landscape of a tribe or kingdom. They were able to enact such change via their mastery and power over one thing in particular: Words.

Words have power, and those who were able to compose words in a specific pattern, and utter such words at the right place, at the right time, were inherently powerful. The bards drew upon a somewhat mystical force known as *Awen*, a force which flowed from the depths of the Otherworld into our own world. Poetry touched by the *Awen* not only had the power to move people and communities on a visceral level but could also be elevated to prophecies which foretold what was to come of great rulers, mighty kingdoms, and the culture of the landscape on the whole.

One of the greatest and most revered prophetic poets is likely the legendary figure that is Taliesin. The radiant brow, who lore explains was born after a thrilling magical event which featured the Witch Goddess Cerridwen, and a boy named Gwion Bach who had drank three mystical drops from her cauldron, which was meant for Cerridwen's son. With the power of these three mystic drops Gwion Bach is given mystical powers and foresight, and so he transforms into various prey animals to escape the wrath of the Witch. Alas, Cerridwen takes the form of various predators and pursues Gwion across the land. Eventually Gwion transforms himself into a grain of wheat, and Cerridwen, with the intention of destroying him, transforms herself into a large, black, speckled hen and gobbles him up.

The magic of the cauldron is too strong, however, and rather than dying within Cerridwen's stomach, Gwion, in the form of a seed, transforms into a foetus and grows in Cerridwen's womb. Eventually, he is reborn, and Cerridwen cannot bring herself to destroy him, and so she sets him into the Otherworldly waters in a coracle. Eventually he is fished out of the waters and as his finders unwrap him from the coracle his brow shines radiantly. He is now Taliesin.

This is the story most are likely familiar with when it comes to Taliesin. However, there is far more to Taliesin within Welsh lore than this one story. In fact, within the context of the literary record, this is a rather late folk tale when compared to the other sources regarding this powerful, legendary figure. The story above is part of a greater text recorded in a 16th century manuscript, Elis Gruffydd's *Chronicle*. Taliesin's name, however, can be traced in the written record as far back as the 9th century.

The earliest record we have of Taliesin can be found in the *Historia Brittonum* (The History of the Britons). A 9th century manuscript, here Taliesin is briefly mentioned in a list of the well-regarded historical poets of Britain. He is described as a

6th century poet who sang the praises of a King in the region of what is now Northumbria (Williams, 2021).

Throughout various pieces of Welsh lore, be it poetry, prose, triad, or otherwise, Taliesin seems to appear often and is almost always regarded as a chief bard, a great poet, a wise prophet, an all-knowing being. He appears in myths such as *How Culhwch won Olwen* and *Branwen ferch Llŷr*. An entire Welsh manuscript now known under the title of *The Book of Taliesin* contain various poems attributed to him. If anyone could don the title of being *the* poet of the Welsh tradition, it is Taliesin.

Scholars such as the great Sir Ifor Williams have long discussed the idea that there were likely two Taliesin's. The first being a historical figure, likely a poet or bard from around the late 6th century who sang the praises of his King. The second is the mythical or mystical Taliesin, a legendary being who is a shape-shifter, a wizard, a prophet, a seer, born from the Cauldron of Awen, he who sings the songs of the past and delivers the prophecies of the future.

Either way, in whatever form he appears, poetry is the one thing that seems to tie all versions of Taliesin that may exist together. Whether he be a human being singing the praises of his lord in court, or a prophetic entity filled with the knowledge of all of creation, his primary art is always poetry and song.

He is not the only great legendary figure who is tied to both magic and poetry. For in Welsh tradition these two arts seem to meld and exist as one and the same. Even the great Myrddin, aka Merlin, who is known today as a mighty sorcerer, has his origins in Welsh texts as a bard or prophetic poet. And so, it only makes sense that we might turn to poetry to inform our understanding of the divine within a Welsh cultural context. One source we might turn to are the poems of *The Book of Taliesin*.

The Book of Taliesin is the title given to a medieval Welsh manuscript containing over sixty poems attributed to Taliesin himself. The poems contained within the manuscript are songs of great Kings, prophecies, elegies, riddles, and even a few brain teasers. This is but one of several Welsh manuscripts containing interesting poetry.

Our poetry contains information pertaining to mythologies, legends, prophecies, histories, and genealogies. By exploring the ancient poetry of Wales, we can glean further information regarding the entities we might revere as Deities today. Several poems make reference to the characters found in the *Mabinogi* and other prose tales and can offer us a deeper insight into the perception the Welsh have had of such characters over the centuries.

Beyond simply looking at medieval poetry, even poetry from the early modern period and onwards can provide us with a depth of information that may otherwise be overlooked. The poems of the likes of Dafydd ap Gwilym, and even later folk songs can provide us with a glimpse of the ever-present nature of the Bardic Tradition of Wales. Do not dismiss poetry in your study of Welsh Deities.

Folklore

Every region across Wales has its own collection of *Straeon Gwerin*, Folk Tales. These are the stories of local Witches, ghostly hauntings, fairy encounters, magical musical instruments, hidden treasures, and whimsical characters. On occasion certain names might appear in folk tales which would ring familiar to those with an interest in Welsh Deities. Whether it be Gwyn ap Nudd riding across the skies over *Cadair Idris* at Halloween, a reef out to sea from Caernarfon Bay being the fabled home of the Goddess Aranrhod, stones along the shores of *Llyn Tegid* being named the fingers of Cerridwen, or entire towns being named after Taliesin.

Folklore is yet another source we can turn to in order to glean information of the Deities of Wales. However, before we begin to touch on folklore, we must ask ourselves, what exactly is the difference between folklore and mythology anyway?

There is no objectively agreed upon definition as to the clear definitive difference between folklore and mythology. Various scholars, folklorists, and writers across the centuries have attempted to delineate a clear line between the two fields of study, however, it is clearly a difficult task. What one culture might define as a myth may be a folk tale to another culture.

For example, former professor of classical studies at Indiana University, William Hansen, attempted to draw up a clear difference in his book *Classical Mythology* (Hansen, 2004). Within his definition, a Myth was defined by its alleged historicity. What made something a myth as opposed to a folk tale was that it had a grounding in the real world. A myth, according to Hansen, takes place in a clearly defined time and a clearly defined place. Myths were also incredibly detailed, with characters having specific names, lineages, even potentially genealogies and links to real historical figures.

In contrast, within this definition, folk tales were supposedly far vaguer. Characters in folk tales are often unnamed, the story takes place at an indefinite period of time, and the location is unnamed as well. Folk tales are generic stories, set in generic places, featuring generic characters who might interact with greater mythological characters such as Deities. Folk tales act as a means to illustrate moral principles, whereas myths illustrate the great stories, which may have actually happened, of a nation or people.

This, of course, is all within the context of Hansen's area of study, Classical Mythology. That is, the mythology of ancient Greece and Rome. Perhaps these definitions of mythology and folklore do work within that cultural context (though I am certain several individuals reading this who are more well versed in classical mythology may be disagreeing right now) however, within a Welsh cultural context this doesn't work at all.

Take, for example, the story of the birth of Taliesin as discussed in the section above on poetry. This is a story which is set in a very specific place, at the shores of Llyn Tegid in Bala, North Wales. The characters have very specific names, and some even have links to legendary and potentially historical figures. Whilst many could extract a moral principle woven into the story, the story in and of itself is so incredibly complex that there are numerous ways one might interpret it.

Yet, the story of Taliesin's birth is labelled by most scholars today as a 16th century folk tale, not a myth. Though I am personally aware of several individuals both within the academic field of Celtic Studies and beyond who would disagree with its designation as a folk tale, by and large the story is approached today as an early modern folk narrative.

Perhaps within a Welsh cultural context, then, the difference between a myth and a folk tale is its age? Folk tales are the stories of periods in time within the last thousand or so years, and mythology are the stories of the ancient pre-Christian world? Well, unfortunately this definition would also be redundant within a Welsh context.

Whilst our great prose stories are believed to have remnants of an older mythology which would have been transmitted orally long before the stories were put onto paper, we still have no way to definitively tell just how far back such oral transmissions might have extended. The age of the stories, such as the four branches of the *Mabinogi*, is something that has been the subject of debate for an incredibly long time.

The manuscripts within which the stories we know and adore today are preserved within are dated to approximately the 14th or 15th centuries, however, it is believed the versions recorded in these manuscripts are copies of much older versions (Charles-Edwards, 1996). Scholars of the late 19th and early 20th centuries, such as Sir Ifor Williams, believed the stories came from a period of time around the 11th century, and that they held echoes of an older tradition of mythology which initially were transmitted orally. Other scholars, such as W. J. Gruffydd, believed the versions of the stories we have preserved today are corrupted pieces of mythology. That the stories have their origin in an older pre-Christian culture and that the stories as we know them today are medieval interpretations and adaptations of such myths. Gruffydd sought to theorise what the "original" versions of these stories might have been in his works, though his methods are often criticized by the scholars of today.

By now, many scholars actually shy away from categorising the *Mabinogi* as mythology at all. Celtic Studies researchers and lecturers such as Simon Rodway of Aberystwyth University prefer we instead view the stories as simply 'Welsh Literature', as categorising them as 'Celtic Myths' romanticises them and reduces what truly makes them special into a homogenised Celtic fantasy (Rodway, 2018).

Most dictionaries today define myth as traditional stories, usually involving supernatural or magical beings and events, which hold a prominent role in the culture of a people. By this very broad definition of mythology, I would personally say the *Mabinogi* fits this role perfectly. The *Mabinogi* is part and package of Welsh culture today, the characters, events, and ideas woven into the stories influence our modern literature, music, art, and everyday lived culture. They have held a prominent position in our pride and sense of being for centuries now, and as such, in my personal opinion at least, if they were not classed as myths to begin with, they have certainly been elevated to such a level by today.

But how then might we clearly define the difference between a myth and a folk tale? After all, important Welsh folklorists such as T Gwynn Jones have also labelled the stories of the *Mabinogi* as folk tales. Rather than arguing the difference between mythology and folklore on a broader scale, I will instead provide my own personal definitions of these two words and how I delineate between the two within the context of my own culture's stories.

A myth is a story which holds great cultural relevance to the entire nation. They are stories that have long been preserved in old manuscripts, and as such the canon and lore of such stories are mostly agreed upon on a broader cultural level. Whilst the events of the stories might happen in specific locations across the country, the stories have been embraced by people across all areas where Welsh culture is celebrated.

A folk tale, on the other hand, are regionally specific tales which may not hold much relevance outside of its own square mile (beyond being an entertaining story). Each region might have its own version of similar folkloric motifs, transplanted into their locale. They are the stories of the common people, told in local taverns and pubs, at schools and village halls, churches and corner shops. These stories alter and change with time, and as such do not necessarily always have a clear and unchanged 'canon' to them. They are stories of local features, local characters, and local histories.

Whilst I acknowledge this definition is vague, and that many might disagree with them, these are the definitions we will be working with in the context of this specific book.

Welsh folklore often exists *Ar Lafar* (on the tongue), though over the last couple of centuries numerous individuals have collected and gathered the stories, traditions, customs, and beliefs of certain regions into lovely books. These include the works of T. Gwynn Jones, Elias Owen, John Rhys, Anne Ross, William Rowlands, Evan Isaac, Myrddin Fardd, Marie Trevelyan, and Hugh Evans to name a few. With some doing a better job of it than others according to modern scholars and folklorists. Some of the more modern names we might spot on the shelves of booksellers today include names such as Delyth Badder, Peter Stevenson, Mark Rees, and Miranda Aldhouse-Green. Interest in Welsh folklore seems to rise year after year.

Whilst folk tales, for the most part, provide us with stories of local characters, whimsical fairies, troublesome spirits, or fantastical creatures, occasionally certain names and ideas from the *Mabinogi* and our older literature will get a mention.

The Cŵn Annwn, for example, the hounds of the Otherworld, who we are introduced to in the first branch of the *Mabinogi* are featured in numerous folk tales from across Wales. Often their appearance in folklore matches that which we are given in the *Mabinogi,* hunting hounds with shining white fur and blood-red ears who belong to the King of the Otherworld. Occasionally, however, their nature is altered somewhat. They become more so spectral hounds whose growls and howls echo through the skies as an omen of death (Owen, 1887).

One of the many Kings of the Otherworld we come across in Welsh lore, Gwyn ap Nudd, features in the writings of folklorist T. Gwynn Jones. Via his work we discover that Gwyn ap Nudd has a connection to the region of Corwen, Denbighshire. He is also said to have a connection to owls, and that people might be carried away by owls via his command (Jones, 1930). These are facets of lore relating to Gwyn ap Nudd that would not be immediately apparent were we to simply approach him via his appearances in mythology.

As such, folklore is but one more treasure trove we might dig into in order to learn more about the Deities we might revere today. Folklore provides us with an alternative view of such entities, as within these folk stories and traditions we gain a glimpse of how the common everyday people might have perceived and interacted with such beings. Mythology, such as the four branches of the *Mabinogi,* were stories preserved in manuscripts by the elites, the nobility. It is interesting to note how the same names might appear in both medieval manuscripts and in early modern folk practices or stories, and to acknowledge where such characters might differ in perception.

Chapter 3

Cosmology

One aspect of Welsh lore which many might find frustrating is that we have very little evidence of a fixed and objective cosmology that can be interpreted as an inherently polytheistic or pre-Christian cosmology from the sources we have available. We have no creation myths, no texts that clearly and definitively outline what the Welsh believed our Gods to be, nor even the best way to approach them within a polytheistic lens.

This is primarily because all sources we have available to us are rooted in a period of time when Wales had already embraced Christianity. As we discussed in the previous chapter, even our myths as we know them today are preserved within manuscripts from a heavily Christian era, and so expressed via a Christian world view. With all this in mind, it is difficult to discuss a specifically Welsh cosmology which expresses an authentic, ancient world view relating to Deities, religion, worship, and the way of the world.

What we can do, however, is acknowledge the aspects of our stories which undoubtedly carry an arcane essence or element to them. It is from these aspects of our lore we might decipher at least a portion of a cosmology which relates to how we might once have acknowledged and approached the divine in everyday life.

In a lecture delivered by Professor Ronald Hutton at Gresham College in 2023, Hutton approached the idea of finding remnants of lost Gods and, by extension, hints at pre-Christian mythology within Welsh medieval literature. During his talk he mentioned that there are two specific themes woven into the four branches of the *Mabinogi*. The first is shapeshifting, and the second is *Annwfn* – The Welsh expression of the Otherworld (Hutton, 2023).

In this chapter we will focus primarily on the cosmology and lore surrounding the Otherworld, and by extension certain ideas rooted in Welsh culture that have a tie to the Otherworld. One such idea is the concept of *Awen*, of divine inspiration. By searching down these two avenues primarily we may be able to glean a glimpse at what might have been once an aspect of a greater cosmology.

The Otherworld

There is one force which seems to impact the lore of a variety of Deities and characters from Welsh myth and lore, and that is the Otherworld. Some Deities seem to have come from the Otherworld, whereas others interact with this strange place in a variety of ways. In order to better understand the Gods themselves, it will be beneficial to have an understanding of this Otherworld.

The name given to the Otherworld within the Welsh language is *Annwfn*. You may have also seen it spelled *Annwn*. Both of these spellings are correct, the difference merely being dependant on the sources from which we glean information about the Otherworld. Despite having grown up with the *Annwn* spelling, I now personally prefer the spelling *Annwfn*, and why that is will be illuminated as we explore the cosmology behind the Otherworld.

The Welsh language is an inherently poetic language, as we have already explored. One cannot simply take a word and give it a singular definitive translation. Single words within our language can hold entire stories and cosmologies within them. This is certainly the case with the word *Annwfn*. The word itself can illustrate the beliefs and ideas surrounding what and where the Otherworld is.

Sioned Davies translates *Annwfn* to mean "The in-world" (Davies, 2007). This could be poetically interpreted to mean "the world within our own world". The word itself is composed of two words *An* and *Nwfn,* the former being a prefix which can be used to both intensify and negate within the Welsh language. We see the prefix *An* attached to words such as *hapus* (happy), or *cyfreithlon* (legal), With this prefix attached the words are transformed into antonyms of the original word. *Hapus,* denoting happiness, becomes *Anhapus* denoting misery. *Cyfreithlon,* meaning legal, becomes *Anghyfreithlon* meaning illegal.

However, the prefix *An* can also be attached to words in order to intensify the word. For example, the word *Andros* is often used to denote that something is "very" something, "intensely" something. For example, "*Andros o lwcus*" translates to mean "incredibly lucky".

It is in the latter context many believe the *An* in *Annwfn* should be perceived. The second half of the word *Nwfn* is believed to have derived from the word *dwfn* meaning depth or the deep (Rudiger, 2021). It is for that reason I prefer the spelling *Annwfn,* as it expresses and illustrates the word's relation to the concept of depth better in my opinion. If we put it all together the translation of *Annwfn* could be "The Very Deep/Depths".

By that definition Davies' translation of the word above matches quite well. "The Very Deep" and "The World Within" could be perceived to mean the same thing. There are also countless ways one might interpret both of these translations of the name given to the Otherworld.

A world within, or a place of great depth. On a literal level we could perceive this as meaning a literal place located in "the depths" or "within" our world. A chthonic land, located beneath our feet. Or, alternatively, a land located beneath the waves of the sea, or under great, deep lakes.

This literal interpretation works well with the version of the Otherworld we see expressed in folklore. Often the Otherworld is located beneath our world. In the writings of Giraldus Cambrensis in the 12th century he recounts a tale about a boy who lives among the fair folk in their Otherworldly realm for a period of time. In this tale the Otherworld was accessed via a door located at the banks of a river. The door led the boy to a sub-terranean world, a place not too dissimilar to our world, except that it is in a state of constant twilight due to the lack of sunlight.

In other stories throughout the lore and legend of Wales people find themselves in the Otherworld after falling into lakes, venturing too deep into caves, or even sailing across the deep seas. By these descriptions of the Otherworld, we could certainly make sense of the name *Annwfn* as meaning "The Very Deep" or "The World Within".

However, one could also interpret the meaning of *Annwfn* via a metaphorical lens. Rather than a land literally located in the depths, perhaps *Annwfn* represents the deepening of our reality, and the depth of our being. Whilst perhaps this interpretation might seem a little "airy-fairy" for some, there are instances in traditional lore which could corroborate this line of thinking.

To the bards of ancient Wales *Annwfn* was more than just a fairy land or a place of heroic quests. *Annwfn* was also the birthplace of all poetic inspiration. Those who wished to write profound poetry would hope the Awen would touch them, and the Awen begins its life in the depths of the Otherworld. It is not difficult to look at the Otherworld within this context and to envision that a deeper part of ourselves, the emotional core of our being where poetry and art is born from, is therefore somehow connected to the Otherworld.

In the *Mabinogi*, the Otherworld is not perceived as some far-off land accessible only to magical users or those who stumble upon some kind of portal. On the contrary, Pwyll, when guided by Arawn in the first branch, simply strolls into the Otherworld as though it were just an extension of his own landscape. Similarly, the Otherworld bleeds through into our reality and influences the narrative of the third branch as well.

The Otherworld within its Welsh cultural context is not merely a different dimension or reality within which mythic characters sometimes find themselves. Instead *Annwfn* is always closer than one might initially believe. A constant influence on our world, just a breath away.

Annwfn is also the place of birth of some of the Gods we come across in Welsh lore. If not their place of origin, there are also Deities associated closely with the Otherworld. Rhiannon appears out of the Otherworld, a daughter of a great Lord of a region in what is likely *Annwfn*. Other Deities with connections to the Otherworld include Gwyn ap Nudd, Arawn, Modron, Cerridwen, and Taliesin to name a few.

Beyond Deities, the denizens of the Otherworld are also known as *Y Tylwyth Teg* (The Fair Family) in folklore. The Otherworld is sometimes described as islands located out to sea, and upon these islands live fairy beings who will frequently visit our world.

The Otherworld within Welsh cosmology is a place of plenty. An abundant landscape populated by flamboyant, intriguing entities who live a life of opulence and magic. It is the birthplace of all poetic and prophetic inspiration, a place where great heroes journey to on mighty quests, and sometimes a place of danger.

Awen

The earliest literary record we have of the concept of Awen extends back to the 9th century in the manuscript titled the *Historia Brittonum*. In this manuscript the Awen is merely referenced within the name of a man named Talhaearn Tadawen – Iron brow, the father of Awen. The fact this old text references the Awen in this context implies the concept of Awen was likely already an established aspect of the culture at the time.

Bards would sing of the Awen in their poetry as a mystical force, a spirit which can possess the poet and enable them to birth poetry that is divinely touched, prophetic, and powerful. The chief bard of Welsh lore, Taliesin, was said to have been created by three blessed drops of a distilled potion of the Awen itself.

A medieval poem titled *Angar Kyfundawt* (A Hostile Confederacy of Bards) speaks of the Awen as a force which starts its life in the Otherworld, shaped by divine hands, which then works its way into our reality like an ever-flowing river (Haycock, 2007).

It is interesting that the Awen would hold such mystical connotations. An Otherworldly force which possesses and moves the bard, associated in lore with the cauldron of the great Witch Goddess Cerridwen. It is especially interesting when one considers all literary mentions we have of the Awen stem from a period in Welsh history when Wales had already embraced Christianity. The bards of early Christian Wales sang the praises of the Christian God, but also of the Awen. To the bards, Awen almost appears to be a divinity in and of itself.

Awen plays a vital role in the bardic culture of Wales, but is also, I believe, an important core cosmological facet of the Welsh tradition in a broader sense. Our culture is one of song, poetry, art, prose, and theatrical ceremony. Our Gods are venerated via the arts, we sing of their magic, and it is the Awen which illuminates the inner artist deep within ourselves.

You may have come across the symbol associated with Awen when interacting with modern day Pagan groups, especially modern-day Druids. The symbol mostly associated with the Awen today are the three rays. You may have seen this symbol with three rays pointing downwards, and three dots above said rays. Some would look at this symbol and state it is simply the symbol of Druidry. Others state it is the symbol that represents the Awen. Both of these statements hold truth, yet also miss a rather important point.

Regarding it being the "symbol of Druidry", this is true in that it is utilised and identified as being associated with various

Druidic organisations today. It is likely if you come across an individual who wears the symbol with the three rays and the three dots that they are indeed a Druid. The symbol with the three dots specifically is deeply associated with Druidry.

The original form of this symbol does not feature said dots above the rays. The symbol of the three rays is credited to Welsh visionary (and literary forger) Iolo Morganwg. Its name within Morganwg's work is *Y Nod Cyfrin* (the mystic note). Rather than being a symbolic representation of the Awen itself, Morganwg writes that the three rays instead represent the influence of Awen on our world (Ab Ithel, 2004). The three rays represent the pillars of balance, the three principles which keep our world in a balanced state of being. These principles are love, truth, and knowledge.

The symbol itself is arguably rather modern; however, it represents the influence of a force which can be traced far back into the mists of time. This symbol has been adopted into Welsh culture and is an integral aspect of the Gorsedd tradition, which is the organising body and the beating heart of the National Eisteddfod, the largest cultural festival in Wales. During the National Eisteddfod you will see the symbol of the three rays on banners, ceremonial robes, trophies and chairs, pamphlets and guides, and more. The Gorsedd is composed of what we refer to as "cultural Druids" – all members of the Gorsedd are Druids, but they are not religious Druids per se. The Druids of the Gorsedd can be of any faith, and I know of members today who are Christians, Atheists, and even Pagans. The Gorsedd tradition was also initiated by Iolo Morganwg, and much of modern Druidry draws its foundations from the same bodies of work as this tradition at the heart of modern-day Welsh culture.

This is why the Awen is such an integral aspect of both Welsh culture and also modern Pagan Druidry. They draw upon the same lore and have similar backgrounds when looking at their formation. The symbol of the three rays and the concept of Awen is now a foundational aspect of numerous Druid orders.

However, it must be noted that Druids do not own the concept of Awen.

The Awen can be worked with and called to by anyone. Whether you are a Witch, a Druid, a Christian, a Pagan. The Awen is ever-present in our lives, a flowing force which begins its life in the Otherworld. We breathe it into our bodies, and as it takes hold we then create and birth profound creative, visionary, magical work into the world.

The Awen sings in awe of all of creation, and that song can be heard by keen ears. It echoes upon the breeze, hums in the tides and waves, and beats like a drum in the depths of the mounds of the Earth. It is the heart-song of all of reality itself, and those who seek to hear such a song have the potential to be moved by it.

The Awen acts as a bridge between our mortal existence and the divine.

Exercise: Singing the Awen

If Awen acts as the bridge between us and the divine, then we must embrace its song during our devotional practices. Awen is so deeply connected to breath, spoken word, and song and as such one of the most effective methods of drawing upon its power is to sing in awe of it, and in return it will sing in awe of you.

Here I have outlined a simple exercise you can do at home to draw upon the power of Awen. All one needs to perform this exercise is a safe, quiet space where you will not be disturbed, a comfortable chair, or alternatively a comfortable floor to sit on, and, optionally, a bell might also be useful.

Harkening back to the works of Iolo Morganwg and rooted at the heart of many Druid traditions today is the idea of singing the Awen. There are numerous ways one might do this. One method is to sing vowel sounds. A rather silly and somewhat offensive joke people love to say about the Welsh language is that we "have no vowels". Anglo-centric individuals see placenames such as *Ysbyty Ystwyth* and will laugh about the lack of vowels and how "unpronounceable" such words are. The truth, however, is that the Welsh language actually has more vowels than the English language does. Our vowels are:

A, E, I, O, U, W, Y

Welsh is a phonetic language, and as such the letters in our alphabet are always pronounced the same (minus one or two instances where they might change). In many ways, this makes Welsh somewhat easier than the English language, for the letter 'A' in Welsh will always be pronounced the same, a fact that cannot be said for English where the letter 'A' will have several different pronunciations depending on the context within which it is used. At the back of this book, you can find a guide to Welsh pronunciation. The vowels in Welsh are pronounced as follows:

A – ah, as in the 'a' in 'cat', 'hat', or 'far'.
E – eh, as in the 'e' at the start of words such as 'elevate' or 'embassy'.
I – ee, similar to how one might pronounce the double 'e' in English words such as 'deer'.
O – aw, as in the 'aw' in words such as 'fawn', or 'prawn'.
U – This one is difficult for English speakers. It is similar to an 'ee' sound, but one must curl the tongue into the shape of a 'U'.
W – ooh, as in the double 'o' in words like 'food'.
Y – Uhh, like a longer 'u' sound as in words such as 'fun'.

Vowel sounds open up the vocal cords and are pronounced whilst exhaling, and so we can sing these sounds out and hold them for as long as we are able on a single breath. However, there are specific vowel sounds that have certain magical connotations, and those are:

O, I, W

These vowel sounds are the sound of creation itself. They are the song of the three realms of Land, Sky, and Sea. The vowel sound of O represents sea, I is sky, and W is land. When we sing these vowel sounds we are singing with the joy of creation and the magic of the natural world.

Find yourself seated or stood in a comfortable position. Centre yourself, take a few calming breaths and close your eyes. If it is comfortable for you to do so, pay attention to your posture. If possible, straighten the back, lift the chin slightly skyward, and allow your shoulders to relax and your chest to open up.

Once comfortable and calm, take a deep breath into your diaphragm. When breathing into your core or your diaphragm you should feel your stomach extend as you inhale. Take as deep a breath as possible, and then as you exhale sing with a clear, confident voice the vowel sequence of:

O, I, W

All on one breath. Keep projecting those sounds in a sequence that sounds almost as though you are singing *AWWWW, EEEEEEH, OOOOH* until you no longer have breath left. As your breath runs out, repeat the process and take a deep inhale so as to sing the vowel sounds again. Keep repeating this as many times as necessary.

When done, take a moment to ponder over how that felt. You might find it beneficial to journal about the experience. How did it feel to sing the song of creation? The song of land, sea, and sky? How did your body feel projecting that sequence of sounds? Work with these sounds and sing them as an invocation to draw the Awen into your life. You may wish to incorporate this into a daily devotional rite to the Awen. Ground, centre, breathe, relax, and then inhale before ringing an altar bell and singing the vowel sounds, projecting them out into the air.

Alternatively, if singing the vowels does not quite sit right with you, you could always attempt to instead sing the verb of Awen. If we were to translate the word 'Awen' into English, the best way to do so would be to describe it as 'divine poetic inspiration'. If we dare to reduce this, we might say it is a mystical form of inspiration. If Awen is 'inspiration' then what is its verb? How would one say 'inspire'?

The verb of Awen is simple, it is the same word but with an 'a' added onto the end: *Awena*. It is pronounced: Ah-when-ah.

To sing the verb of Awen, and to draw forth the Awen's inspiring force, you may sing the verb all on one breath.

Ah-when-ah

Follow the instructions above but rather than singing the vowel sounds as you exhale, sing instead the word Awena. Do not worry too much about the tune you sing it to, the most important aspect of this is that you sing the sounds of *AH*, *WHEN*, and *AH* in an open, echoing, manner. Sing with your whole being, lose yourself in the song.

To sing to the Awen is to invoke it, and therefore this exercise can be utilised in a variety of settings. You could perform this exercise as a daily devotional act as already mentioned, as a means of building power in ritual or magic, as a method of invoking Awen in situations where you feel somewhat lost, and even in group settings. I find singing the vowel sounds is truly exhilarating and powerful in a group setting. The sounds of everyone's voice, if they dive into it without limiting the power of their voices, seem to blend into a vibrational hum which energises and empowers all involved. I have partaken in ritual where we have sung the vowel sounds for long periods of time and we all leave in a buzz, as though we have just downed three espressos in a row.

Chapter 4
Magic

Throughout our myths, poetry, and folk tales, magic is simply a part of day-to-day life. Many of our Deities are themselves powerful and learned magical practitioners. Magic is a constant throughout the Welsh cultural continuum, and as such learning to practice the art of enchantment is a powerful and transformative method of connecting with our Gods.

In this chapter we will briefly discuss magic within a mythic context. We will also touch upon magical tools one might turn to in a practice that draws inspiration from the traditions of Wales.

Magic in Mythology

When delving into the magic apparent in Welsh mythology, we have to keep in mind the medieval context within which the stories have been preserved and passed onto us today. In an essay entitled *Magic and Marvels* by Mark Williams in *The Cambridge History of Welsh Literature,* Williams explains how magic was considered a rather dubious force within a medieval context (Williams, 2019).

Whilst magic which involved the conjuring of, and forging of pacts with 'demonic' entities was in the realm of the infernal and sinister, magic which instead drew upon the virtues of stones, herbs, trees, and the movement of the celestial bodies resided in a grey area. This form of natural magic might be seen as existing within the realms of miracle, the Christian God created the natural world so surely, he would occasionally allow us, his children, to work with the wonders of such a world, right?

Magic as it is presented in the four branches of the *Mabinogi* is predominately concerned with the act of transformation.

Magic, in its most basic form within this context, is the ability to change or transform something. The magic of transformation was also split into two categories within these stories.

First, we have the magic that deals with something or someone's *Rhith*. To change something or someone's *Rhith* is to change their outward form. Their appearance. This is the magic of disguise, of illusion. It is skin deep. In the first branch of the *Mabinogi* Arawn transforms the shape or image of himself and Pwyll so that they each look like the other. This is so that Pwyll can live in Arawn's kingdom and be perceived as the ruler of said kingdom, and vice versa. Whilst they have been transformed to look like one another, this is nothing more than an illusion, a glamour, a disguise. Scratch the surface and underneath you will find the person they truly are. Whilst Pwyll looks like Arawn, he is still Pwyll, his core nature remains the same.

In Welsh, when discussing the magical arts, you will see the term *Hud a Lledrith* used often. This is usually translated to mean "magic and enchantment", but it is somewhat more complex than that. The word *Hud* is a complicated one on an etymological level. Some linguists believe it is somewhat related to the Norse word *seiðr*, and that it deals with a cultural form of magic (Williams, 2019).

The word *Lledrith* on the other hand is somewhat easier to deconstruct etymologically. The prefix *Lled* comes from a word denoting 'semi', 'somewhat' or 'half'. The suffix *rith* comes from the word *Rhith,* shape or form. And so *Lledrith* can be translated literally to 'half form' or 'semi shape'. In a more poetic sense, however, it is the magic that sees physical shape and form as malleable.

And then we have the magic that deals with something or someone's *Anian*. That word, *Anian,* denotes something or someone's inner nature, soul, or core. It is who someone is beyond outward appearance. The truest expression of someone's being. It is the anima, as one might put in classical philosophical terms (not to be confused with the psychological idea of the anima as coined by Jung).

When Gwydion and Gilfaethwy are punished and transformed into animals in the fourth branch, it is not merely their *Rhith* that is changed but their *Anian*. Their shape is not simply transformed into the appearance of animals, but they become the animals on a soul level. When we consider how they were transformed into animals (with their sex often changed as well) and 'made to mate', no one was there forcing them to mate in the form of these animals. They mated because they were, at their most fundamental levels, following the very nature of the animals they were changed into. Their instincts, inner nature, and perception of the world was altered to that of the animals.

Other examples of transformative magic in the myths include the transforming of women into mice in the third branch of the *Mabinogi*, the conjuration of Blodeuedd out of the flowers of Oak, Broom, and Meadowsweet in the fourth branch, and the ability of the *Pair Dadeni* (The Cauldron of Rebirth) in the second branch to bring the dead back to a semblance of life.

The witch Goddess Cerridwen had the ability to change her form at will as well, and Gwion Bach, once touched by the Awen, also gained this ability. They change their forms in the blink of an eye, fuelled by their strong emotions. Gwion becomes prey animals, spurred on by his fear and desire to survive. Whereas Cerridwen becomes predators, spurred on by her fury and desire to kill. Even the original intention of Cerridwen's magic in this story is at its core a desire to transform something. She seeks to create a potion of pure, distilled Awen so that her hideous son will at the very least have the most profound, prophetic, inspiring mind.

It is interesting that the majority of these stories as they have been handed down to us exist with a veneer of Christian cosmology layered over them. Despite that veneer, magic is rarely seen as an inherently wicked skill or art, instead magic within Welsh myth appears to be neutral, its nature only tainted by the nature of its user. Magic can be used to harm, but also to heal. Even some of the great rulers in the *Mabinogi* are magicians, such as Math fab Mathonwy, King of Gwynedd in the fourth branch.

Magic is often presented via two different expressions, there is Otherworldly magic and also magic practiced by Earthly magicians. The magic of the Otherworld tends to be subtle and part of the Otherworldly denizens' very nature. There is no fanfare or ritual behind Rhiannon's usage of magic in the first branch, though it is clear magic seems to surround her. Whereas the magic practiced by mortals seems to carry an air of ceremony and learned skill behind it. Gwydion and Math are not from the Otherworld, they are part of a dynasty of rulers based in Gwynedd. Their magic is rooted in their mastery of words and their connection to the landscape around them. They use magical wands to cast their spells, gather flowers and woods from the land around them, and, at least in Gwydion's case, have a mastery over the bardic arts as well.

The connection between magic and the spoken word coincides well with the beliefs surrounding the concept of Awen, as discussed in the previous chapter, as well as the history concerning the Welsh tradition of poetry as discussed in the Chapter 2. Words hold power, and those who weave words in specific ways are inherently powerful. The magician, the bard, and the *Cyfarwydd* (Storyteller) are all essentially one and the same in Wales.

Magical Tools

Those who weave magic in our stories sometimes use specific tools to aid their art. The two most commonly used tools of magic within our myths and lore are the wand and the cauldron.

Cauldrons have long been important vessels for peoples of various cultures across the world. They are often the heart of the community in ancient cultures, acting as the primary feasting vessel. Gatherings would have been held around the cauldron which hung over hot flames, boiling the food of the people. Laughter and joy, marriages and unions, debates and reconciliations would have been held around the cauldron.

And yet, in modern times we tend to think of the cauldron primarily within the context of magic. The image of the fantasy witch is usually attached to the visual of a sinister, bubbling cauldron where she stirs and brews her concoctions and potions. This tradition of associating the cauldron with magic seems to harken back through the ages, as even our oldest stories feature cauldrons utilised in acts of magic, or cauldrons that have their own specific abilities.

There is the cauldron of Cerridwen, which enables her to brew a potion of pure Awen. The story of *Culhwch ac Olwen* refers to a cauldron belonging to an Irish man, Diwrnach Wyddel, and is one of the items Culhwch must acquire in order to gain permission from the giant Ysbaddaden to marry his daughter, Olwen. In the second branch of the *Mabinogi* we are introduced to the *Pair Dadeni,* a magical cauldron which has the ability to reanimate the corpses of fallen warriors, so that they may continue to fight. Brân became the keeper of that particular cauldron after the giants Cymidei Cymeinfoll and Llasar Llaes Gyfnewid gifted it to him, and ultimately Brân gifts it to the Irish King Matholwch in order to reconcile the conflict brought on by his half-brother, Efnysien. In the poem *The Spoils of Annwfn* the great King Arthur goes on a quest into the Otherworld, and here we see yet another cauldron, the cauldron which belongs to the Lord of Annwfn. This cauldron is kindled by the breath of nine maidens and is described as having a dark trim and being adorned with pearls. This cauldron, similar to another cauldron from Welsh lore belonging to the giant Dyrnwch will not boil the food of a coward.

We see the cauldron taking on a variety of guises and forms in Welsh myth and lore, and yet similar motifs tend to remain consistent throughout these depictions. Cauldrons usually play a ceremonial role, or are the component of a great quest or task. Whether that be the quest to become a fine and brave warrior, to marry the one who you love, or to complete a magical spell or rite. The cauldron often has a guardian, usually a giant or a witch. One thing, however, is always certain – the cauldron is a vessel of great transformation. With the help of Cerridwen's cauldron in *Ystoria Taliesin* Gwion Bach transforms from a normal boy to a being who is imbued with the knowledge of all things past, present, and future. The *Pair Dadeni* transforms the corpses of the dead back into living, animate bodies, albeit a shell of their former selves, unable to speak. Some cauldrons will not boil the food of a coward, in an almost initiatory rite for warriors. Transformation and initiation seem a common motif surrounding the cauldron within a Welsh cultural context.

In my work as a *Swynwraig*, a modern Welsh Witch, the cauldron is one of the primary tools of my craft. Not only can it act as a symbolic representation of the magic, myth, and lore of my culture and landscape, but it also has an abundance of practical uses and applications within operative magic.

The cauldron acts as a container for ritual items on my journey to whichever space I might be carrying out my rites. I can use it to cook in, to blend oils and salves together, to burn incense, to safely build a fire within, to carry liquid, to divine within, or even to place offerings within. Within ceremony and ritual, the cauldron can act as a central point, a point of magical transformation, of change and creation. Within my devotional work, I associate the cauldron with a plethora of Deities. The two primary Deities are Brân and Cerridwen, in their roles as keeper of great, legendary cauldrons.

Many are the uses of the cauldron within modern practice for the Welsh Polytheist, Pagan, or magical practitioner. A primary tool in our craft and work, and an incredibly practical one at that.

In the Welsh language we have many terms to describe the vessel that is the cauldron. The two most common you might come across are *Pair* and *Crochan*. The latter is more commonly used in colloquial settings today, whereas the former is the word you are more likely to come across within the context of myth and lore. On a personal level I use both of these words to denote the two different functions of the cauldron.

Pair – A ceremonial cauldron, which acts as a vessel for ritualistic and formal activity. Within this context the cauldron is often symbolic, or the centrepiece for a particular rite, ritual, or ceremony. It is the vessel which burns the sacred herbs, holds the sacred flame, or contains the sacred waters that are central to the work being carried out. For ceremonial forms of magic and ritual.

Crochan – The practical cauldron, which acts as a vessel for hands-on work to be carried out. Within this context the cauldron is a workable tool and vessel. It is the vessel in which herbs are mixed, salves, balms, potions, and elixirs are formed, food is cooked within. For hands-on, operative forms of magic and craft. No need for grand ceremony to use the cauldron in this context, you could be mixing a concoction within it whilst relaxing in your rocking chair and listening to the radio. For folk magical uses, and mundane tasks.

The wand is another tool which holds a prominent presence within Welsh myth and lore concerning magic. Tools predominately utilised by magicians such as Gwydion and Math. The word for a wand in Welsh is *hudlath* which translates, rather poetically, to mean 'a yard of magic'. In the fourth branch of the *Mabinogi,* we see Math and Gwydion utilise their wands for a variety of magical purposes. Interestingly, in modern times we tend to visualise the wand as a delicate, ethereal item, swished about elegantly by Fairy Godmothers, yet in Welsh myth their use is often far more heavy-handed. When Math uses his wand to change the very *anian* of Gwydion and Gilfaethwy into that of animals, he does not swish it about elegantly. Oh no, in these instances Math strikes the boys across their head. A magical, transformational bonk on the head.

The wand acts as an extension of the magician's body, and also as a tether between those who weave magic and the natural world. In the poem *The Battle of the Trees* Gwydion raises an army of trees via his mastery of words, and connection to the land which surrounds him. All the while utilising his one tool in the process – his wand.

A wand, made from the wood of a tree from our own landscape, not only connects us with one specific tree, but with the magic which connects every tree within that species, and all of the trees in the forest. The utilisation of a wand in our magical work not only reminds us of our own power but also reminds us that we are in constant relationship with the world surrounding us. A world that is inherently animate, alive and pulsating. We are not separate from the natural world, we are part of it.

Within my own practice I tend to make the majority of the wands I work with magically. I will connect with a tree for a period of time, before carefully cutting a branch to carve into a wand. Offerings are made to the tree, and I choose the tree carefully for the task I wish to accomplish with the aid of a wand. And so, the wand is another primary tool within the craft and work of a Welsh Polytheist, Pagan, or magical practitioner.

The wand can also aid us in connecting with Deities that are associated with such tools in our lore, or Deities which are magicians. Whether that be Math, Gwydion, or Myrddin to name a few. Math is referenced in the Triads as being the one who taught Gwydion the art of enchantment (Bromwich,

2014), and as such he is a powerful ally to work with for the aspiring practitioner of magic. A divine mentor as we begin to incorporate magic into our everyday lives.

To become a weaver of magic is to enter into a continuum of practice that harkens back to our oldest stories and lore. It enables us to connect more intimately with many Deities within the Welsh pantheon. If you would like to learn more about how to incorporate a magic that sings of the Welsh cultural continuum, I recommend picking up a copy of my debut book, *Welsh Witchcraft*.

Chapter 5

Apotheosis

When approaching the Deities of Wales, there is always one question that haunts us. Are the Welsh Gods truly Gods? One new to the subject might be perplexed by such a question, of course, they are Gods! Aren't they? It may be a shock to hear that this is indeed an ongoing debate. The answer to such a question, of course, depends on what exactly we mean by 'are they Gods?'.

In the introduction to this book, I added a disclaimer that I am not writing this book from an academic perspective, but from the perspective of a modern-day Polytheist, and practitioner of magic. The reason I felt the need to add such a disclaimer is because the way in which we, as modern-day polytheists, pagans, witches etc. approach the material we have spoken about in this book can sometimes be considered controversial in the eyes of academics who view the materials purely as medieval literature and nothing else. The notion that these texts preserved in medieval manuscripts carry an echo of an ancient belief system is one that causes some to recoil in anger or roll their eyes in humorous disbelief.

What are the arguments for and against the idea that characters such as Rhiannon, Gwyn ap Nudd, Aranrhod, or Manawydan are or are not Gods then? That is precisely what we will explore in this section. And buckle up, for this is likely the chapter where I share some of my more controversial and unpopular opinions on this topic.

Are the Welsh Gods *Actually* Gods?

During the introduction to her translation of the Taliesin poem titled *Kadeir Kerrituen* (The Chair of Cerridwen) in *Legendary*

Poems from the Book of Taliesin, Marged Haycock describes Cerridwen as a woman who is clearly a distributor of poetic inspiration. However, she states that Cerridwen cannot be perceived as a Goddess, and her reasoning for this is due to the fact we have no evidence of a cult dedicated to the Goddess Cerridwen (Haycock, 2007).

This seems to be the primary argument against the notion that any characters found within the texts we refer to as Welsh Mythology are Deities. It is true, we have no evidence that anyone ever worshipped the great Goddess Cerridwen, Rhiannon, or Aranrhod. There is no ancient cult of Gwydion, no shrines that survive from the pre-Christian past dedicated to Lleu Llaw Gyffes or Amaethon fab Dôn. The texts themselves which detail the stories and lives of these characters never once refer to them as Gods. To many these names are simply the names of medieval literary characters from the earliest Welsh traditions of literature. Brân is no more a God than Juliet from Shakespeare's *Romeo and Juliet* is a Goddess within this context.

There are two primary issues with this approach, however. The first is that while it is true there is no evidence for any cults or veneration of the characters from, for example, the *Mabinogi* as Gods, there is evidence that some characters carry echoes of something older. Most scholars who write on the *Mabinogi* today are clear that these stories existed in some form or another in an oral tradition of storytelling long before they were ever put to the page (Davies, 2007). How far back those stories that were passed down orally extend, however, is a question we may never know the answer to. Perhaps they do carry echoes of an older corpus of mythology which predates the arrival of Christianity to these shores, or perhaps they do not. The stories at the very least seem to take place in an ancient past, in a time of magic, of great Kings, and a time before the landscape was riddled with invading forces.

There is also the matter of characters bearing names which are cognate with the names of ancient Pagan Deities. Even the staunchest academic who firmly believes that medieval Welsh prose tales are but pieces of great medieval literature cannot argue that names such as Mabon and the ancient God Maponos are unrelated. Whilst we may not find any evidence for a cult dedicated to Nudd, we can say with certainty that there was a temple dedicated to Nodens, whose name is remarkably similar.

We also cannot pin the blame of assuming characters from Welsh mythology are the Gods of ancient Britain on modern day Polytheists and spiritual individuals alone. This notion did not spring up out of nowhere, for until fairly recently this was the common belief some scholars took. Popular scholars, folklorists, and writers on the subject of Welsh literature and folklore such as John Rhys, W.J. Gruffydd, Edward Anwyl, and J.A. MacCulloch all expressed the theory that the characters present in the *Mabinogi* were likely the echoes of pre-Christian Deities. Even more recent scholars such as Patrick Ford and Gwilym Morus-Baird delve into this idea as well.

The fact is these ideas have been present in the works of important, somewhat respected figures for decades. One can hardly blame those with no academic background in such topics not to assume those who do are incorrect, or that the information is outdated. I have a personal disliking of those who sit in their ivory towers, looking down upon those of us who are not as learned, informed, educated, or intelligent as they are, whilst offering no solutions. My question to academics who turn their nose up at those "getting it wrong" is simple: *What are you personally doing to make the "correct" information more accessible to the greater public?* We cannot be sneering at those who "get it wrong" if the "correct" information is only accessible behind extortionate paywalls, flowery inaccessible language that is difficult to decipher, or buried in places the average person with a passing interest in Welsh lore are unlikely to look.

Unless we are of the belief that only those privileged enough to undertake expensive and time-consuming degrees are allowed to interact with this material? An attitude I personally find backwards, offensive, and abhorrent.

The second, and most primary issue in my opinion, is that the arguments against the characters woven into Welsh mythology being Deities exist solely within the context of the past. Yes, it is true there are no shrines from the ancient world dedicated to the Goddess Cerridwen, however, I can point you to an entire temple dedicated to her that sits in the centre of Bala today. No, there is no ancient cult of the Goddess Rhiannon that we know of, but I can point you to several covens and polytheistic groups who revere Rhiannon as a Goddess today.

There can be no argument that these characters have not been elevated to divine status in the modern world, for there is bountiful evidence to prove that they have. When discussions arise regarding the divine status of Welsh mythical beings, the process of apotheosis and the way in which these entities are interacted with via a modern lens is largely ignored or overlooked.

Apotheosis can be defined as the process of elevating something or someone to divine status. The word itself derives from the Greek *apotheoun* which means "to make a God of". Apotheosis describes the process of how something, over time, providing that a need exists for it, can become divine and an inherently important aspect to a group of people's religious and spiritual beliefs and practices. This process has been carried out for millennia across the world and is part of very many spiritual and religious traditions. It may seem odd to us, in our heavily Christian society, to fully understand it. However, polytheistic cultures have elevated things and people to divine status for thousands of years.

I would argue this is exactly what has happened with the characters we see featured in Welsh mythology. Whilst arguments could be made that we do have some pieces of evidence to hint at the possibility of these characters carrying an echo of divinity within them, the fact is that does not matter. Within a modern context, they are now Gods with thousands upon thousands of devotees praying to them, calling to them in ritual and magical practice, and dedicating shrines, temples, and works of art in their honour.

An argument I often come across when discussing the veneration of Welsh Deities among modern polytheistic, pagan, and spiritual groups today is the idea that much of this type of work stems from outside of the culture, and therefore is inherently offensive and dehumanising. It is true that new-age authors with no connection to Wales have long dug into aspect of Welsh culture in order to inject their very modern practices with a sense of authentic 'Celtic' identity. Often the Welsh language and the myths themselves are misrepresented, ripped from their cultural context, and treated as an exotic, romanticised, mystical themes to weave into spiritual traditions which likely also appropriate elements from other cultures at the same time.

The best example of this being done is in the naming of the Autumn Equinox as 'Mabon' within contemporary Paganism. Mabon is the name of a character in Welsh mythology, and he has no association with the autumn equinox at all. The naming of the equinox as 'Mabon' was done so by a California-based Wiccan who clearly had little to no understanding nor appreciation for the culture he was pulling from when he did so (more on this in the 'Mabon' section in Part II). Alas, the designation of the name 'Mabon' onto the neo-pagan wheel of the year has now been cemented into popular pagan culture of today. You are unlikely to find depictions of the 'Wheel of the Year' without the Autumn Equinox being labelled 'Mabon', despite the fact many Welsh individuals, me included, have voiced our discomfort with such an obvious appropriation.

When Welsh voices bring up these issues within Pagan communities today, we are often dismissed, argued with, or even called 'bullies' for daring to speak on our own culture. And so yes, I agree, there are many Anglo-centric individuals who have twisted and warped these stories and characters which are important aspects of our culture to feed their spiritual desires. I truly believe there is room to critique and deconstruct this type of approach, especially if it is in any way harmful towards the culture from which they draw upon.

However, there are also countless Welsh voices and groups who interact with this material within a magical, polytheistic, or spiritual context. Personally, I find the notion that Welsh individuals, who grew up immersed in Welsh culture, who just so happen to also identify as pagans, polytheists, witches etc. should not be allowed to engage with this material incredibly silly. They are our stories too, part and package of our culture.

Speaking on a personal level, I grew up within a Welsh speaking community, undertook my schooling entirely via the medium of the Welsh language up until I left for university. I spent many years reading the stories of the *Mabinogi* in school, partaking in theatrical interpretations of the stories, playing as the characters on the playground, and begging my mother to read me the stories before bed at night. They are my stories, part and package of my upbringing, my heritage, my culture. I was raised in Aberffraw, which according to the second branch of the *Mabinogi* is where Branwen was married. These stories were not merely 'stories' to me, they were, and are, an integral aspect of who I am. Beyond all this I also grew up marginalised, as a queer person, and it was these stories, and elements of my culture's myth and lore which were often my anchor in life. It was my relationship to Cerridwen, Rhiannon, Brân, and Aranrhod as Deities which kept me alive at a period in my life when I felt as though my existence was nothing but a burden upon the world.

I am sure countless modern-day pagans, polytheists, witches, etc. who grew up in Wales feel the same way as I do. In fact, I know many do. When I gather with the Anglesey Druid Order at the shores of Llyn Tegid for our annual pilgrimage in honour of the Goddess Cerridwen, some of the best conversations I have are with fellow Welsh speakers who have also found empowerment and a sense of pride via our Gods.

The *Mabinogi,* and much of our corpus of mythology, folklore, folk customs and beliefs, should not, in my opinion, be reserved for academics alone. They should not be locked in the past either, allowed to stagnate and rot in a sense of antiquity. These stories, the Deities we revere, they are alive and speaking to people today. Whether that be via the novels produced by writers inspired by such tales, the artworks adorning the galleries across Wales, or the songs sung within a ritual circle held by modern day Druids at the shores of Llyn Tegid. They are alive. They are divine. And so yes, the Welsh Gods truly are Gods within the context of this book and my work. That is not to say there are those out there who will disagree with me, I know for a fact many do.

Chapter 6

Seasonal Celebrations

We cannot be certain how the Pre-Christian inhabitants of Brythonic Celtic Britain marked their seasonal calendars. Did they have special times of year to honour their Gods, mark the changing of the seasons, venerate their ancestors, and gather in celebration? It is almost certain they did. Celebration is, after all, an inherently human trait. However, there is very little we can go off of with absolute certainty as to the calendar of revelry within this landscape prior to the arrival of Christianity.

Some ancient monuments are specifically built seemingly with the ability to mark auspicious days throughout the year. For example, Bryn Celli Ddu, a prehistoric landmark located on the Isle of Anglesey is aligned beautifully with the rising sun on the summer solstice. Every year, if the weather is clear enough, the rays of the rising sun penetrate into the chambered tomb, illuminating the inside and bathing it with a glorious golden light. No one knows for certain why the rising of the solstice sun was important. Perhaps it is simply a mundane reason, such as a method for the early farming communities of prehistoric Britain to measure the passage of time. Or perhaps the site and the summer solstice held ceremonial purposes within the cultures of the people who dwelled in this place so many, many years ago.

There are, however, certain times of year that are marked as particularly auspicious and magical within our mythology, folklore, and folk traditions. There are some who believe that aspects of these traditions likely survive from a time long before Christianity was the primary faith of these Isles, but regardless of if that is true or not, they have certainly become important to us in recent centuries.

Three special nights seem to rise above the rest in Welsh tradition. These nights are often referred to as *Y Tair Ysbrydnos* (The Three Spirit-nights). It was during these special, liminal points in the year that the boundaries that may exist between the seen and unseen worlds, the natural and the supernatural, the mundane and the magical, were removed entirely. During these times significant events may occur, contact between our world and the Otherworld was more likely to happen, and sightings of spectres, spirits, and fairies were far more common than at any other time of year.

The first *Ysbrydnos* was Calan Mai, the second was Gŵyl Ganol Haf, and the third was Calan Gaeaf. In this section we will explore these three spirit nights, discuss methods of observing and celebrating them today, and, of course, delve into the connections between these celebrations and our Gods. We will also touch upon significant events within modern Druidry which draw upon Welsh tradition.

Calan Mai

May Day, the start of May. In the traditional Welsh folk calendar summer began at the start of the month of May. An alternate, and possibly older name for Calan Mai was Calan Haf (Owen, 1959). The word *Calan* translates to mean 'the calends of', or simply 'the beginning of/first day of'. Mai is the Welsh for May, and so Calan Mai would be 'The First Day of May'. Haf is Welsh for the season of Summer, and so Calan Haf is 'The beginning of Summer'.

This was a joyous time of year, when the days were growing longer, and those longer days were warmer than the oppressive darkness and colder nights that have just passed. Whilst on one hand this was a busy time for those who worked the land, that hard work was framed by frivolity, ceremony, and merriment. It was at the start of May that farmers in Wales hired farm servants from their local communities to come and help work the fields, tend to livestock and crops, and to aid in the harvesting of the bounties to come. These servants would work tirelessly from May through to the start of November. However, their evenings were often spent amidst their community atop hills and in village greens. The community would gather together to enjoy music, dancing, sports and games, and all manners of merriment. A time of labour and mirth ahead, and it all commenced with the celebration of Calan Mai.

There was also, of course, magic in the air at this time of year. The celebration of Calan Mai or Calan Haf began the evening before May 1st. From when the sun would set on the night before May 1st began Nos Galan Mai or Nos Galan Haf – "The eve of summer". This was a liminal time, a time of transition. Gone were the dark days, and ahead were days of light. This betwixt and between time was believed to be powerful within a magical sense. Spirits of the dead wandered the Earth, the fair folk gathered to dance in circles in hidden locations across the countryside, and at this time it was possible to divine details pertaining to the future.

This magical quality of Nos Galan Haf is echoed in our mythology. May Eve is the only date that is really ever mentioned in our myths. Some of the significant events of the first branch of the *Mabinogi* occur during the eve of summer. In *Culhwch ac Olwen* it is said that every May Day Gwyn ap Nudd fights in an annual battle that will repeat every year on the same day until the end of time against Gwythyr ap Greidol. In the story of *Lludd and Llefelys* a horrid shrieking sound is heard every May Eve, which we later discover is the sound of two mighty dragons battling in the sky – a story connected with the mighty red dragon on our flag.

It seems that even our oldest stories echo the notion that this is an auspicious and liminal time of year, when magical and profound events are likely to occur. As such, it is the perfect time of year to observe for the modern-day Polytheist, Pagan, or magical practitioner hoping to connect with the Deities of Wales.

Exercise: Coelcerth Nos Galan Haf Ritual

As well as the gatherings of merriment held at this time of year, a tradition found in some parts of Wales was to build a *coelcerth* or bonfire. The method of building these fires was rather ritualised. Nine men would be sent to gather nine different types of wood from nine types of trees. The wood gathered would act as fuel for the fire which would be built. Various traditions surrounding leaping over the flames abounded. In some regions, if disease had been found among a flock of sheep or herd of cattle, a sacrificial lamb or calf was thrown onto the flames in hopes that by some magic that would ward the rest of the livestock from the disease. I am certain most of you reading this book would rather not throw a lamb or calf onto a flame, however, we can draw inspiration from the traditions of the past to create new practices or rituals for today.

Here is an outline of a *Coelcerth Nos Galan Haf* (Summer's eve bonfire) ritual. There are two methods of performing this ritual, the first is if you are able to light a fire, the second is if you are not. These could easily be adapted for a group to do together, and you can colour the bare bones of this ritual with invocations to your chosen Deities, or whatever else you so wish. Take this outline as nothing but inspiration and ensure you make it your own.

Method 1

1. On the day of Nos Galan Haf (the eve of May, the last day of April) head to a wooded area in your locale and gather nine different types of wood. Ensure the wood is dry, ready for drying. If it is a particularly wet April perhaps it is best to gather the wood beforehand and dry them indoors first.
2. Build yourself a bonfire, or even a small fire in your fireplace or fire pit as you normally would. Don't use the wood gathered just yet!

3. Take a piece of paper and write a list of things you would like to banish from your life. For example, you might write down that you wish to banish anxieties and fears that are holding you back, particular people who drain you and cause you harm. Whatever you so wish, if you want it gone, write it down.
4. Choose a sacrifice. You could sacrifice your time and craft something, such as a small calf or lamb out of crochet, or clay. Or perhaps you could bake a cake or loaf of bread. Alternatively, you could sacrifice something meaningful to you that you believe is time to let go of…such as that favourite jumper that no longer fits.
5. Tie the piece of paper onto your sacrificial object with a piece of twine or a ribbon.
6. Place the nine woods onto the fire, wait for them to catch fire.
7. Once the wood is burning, take three deep breaths and visualise that as you exhale the things you have written on your list are being blown away by a breeze. Then, throw your sacrificial object with the list attached onto the fire. Watch as it burns and acknowledge that it is time to let go of that which no longer serves you.
8. Keep the ashes from the fire in a jar and place the jar somewhere in your home where it will remain safe and undisturbed for a year. The ashes will protect you and bring you luck and prosperity for the year ahead. Throw away the ashes next May Eve and replace with a new batch.

Method 2

1. Gather together nine different herbs that are important to you. Ensure they are all safe to burn as incense. For a more potent mixture, gather the herbs directly from your locale.

2. Once the herbs of your choice are gathered and dried, on Nos Galan Haf mix together equal parts of each individual herb and crush them together in a mortar and pestle to create one singular incense blend made from your nine sacred herbs.
3. Take a piece of paper and write a list of things you would like to banish from your life. For example, you might write down that you wish to banish anxieties and fears that are holding you back, particular people who drain you and cause you harm. Whatever you so wish, if you want it gone, write it down.
4. Choose an offering for the Gods and spirits of this sacred time. Perhaps you could use a favourite drink or food item as an offering. Tailor the offering for the spirits, Deities, and spiritual allies you tend to work with.
5. Get two fire safe dishes, cauldrons, containers, or bowls. In one of your fire safe containers, light a charcoal disc. In the other place your piece of paper with your list, folded a few times to make it smaller.
6. Pour your incense mixture onto the charcoal disc and allow the scent of the mixture to fill the air around you.
7. take three deep breaths and visualise that as you exhale the things you have written on your list are being blown away by a breeze. Then, place your offering between the two fire safe containers.
8. Finally, if safe to do so, light the piece of paper on fire and let it burn. If you cannot burn the paper, then pour water over it and allow those things written down to be drowned out of existence.
9. Keep the ashes from the incense you burned in a jar and place the jar somewhere in your home where it will remain safe and undisturbed for a year. The ashes will protect you and bring you luck and prosperity for the year ahead. Throw away the ashes next May Eve and replace with a new batch.

Due to its liminal nature, and its appearance in many folk tales and myths, we can easily associate this time of year with various Deities. Nos Galan Haf and Calan Haf are both associated with Otherworldly forces, and as such any Deity associated with the Otherworld can be honoured at this time. Gwyn ap Nudd, Arawn, and Rhiannon are some examples that spring to mind. Rhiannon's son, Pryderi, was also said to be born at this time of year, and so he and his mother can be honoured at the start of summer. Other Deities I might suggest for this time include: Blodeuedd, in her floral maiden form, as this is a time when the landscape is coloured by the sight of blooming flowers. Amaethon, as the divine agriculturalist, God of tending to the fertile landscape. Olwen, Dôn, and Lleu Llaw Gyffes are also all good choices due to their solar, floral, land-based, or Venusian qualities as well.

Gŵyl Ganol Haf

The term *Gŵyl Ganol Haf* translates to mean 'the feast/festival of midsummer'. This is the high point of the lighter half of the year, when the days are at their longest. Around the time of the Summer Solstice.

Being the second *Ysbrydnos* of the year, this is once again a time of liminality and magic. Divination was carried out at this time of year, specifically divination which dealt with the realms of love. Women would carry out divinatory practices to reveal the names or images of their future husbands.

Midsummer was also an opportune time to purify, bless, and ward the home. The two most prominent herbs gathered at this time were St. John's Wort, and the common Mugwort. Tradition stated that the best time to gather them were either at midnight on the eve of Midsummer, or at noon on Midsummer day (Owen, 1959). The herbs gathered at midnight on the eve of Midsummer were said to be potent in breaking curses, keeping away any baneful magics cast upon you, and warding the home from malevolent spirits. Those gathered at noon on Midsummer day itself were said to be good for purifying the home of any stagnant and baneful forces that had gathered throughout the year. Once gathered, sprigs of the Mugwort or St. Johns Wort were hung above entryways into the home.

The sacred tree of the Midsummer was the Birch, and some communities across Wales, particularly the Glamorgan area, erected a *Fedwen Haf* (Summer Birch). The *Fedwen Haf* was comparable to a May Pole, made of birch wood and adorned in colourful ribbons and wreaths. Dancing would take place around the pole and partake in other joyful activities of the summer.

As the summer solstice marks the longest day of the year, the height of the sun's power, it is an opportune time to venerate Deities that are solar in nature or connected with the realms of sky. Lleu Llaw Gyffes, Penarddun, Beli Mawr, and even Arthur who is a Deity associated with strength and power.

Calan Gaeaf

Likely the spookiest of the three spirit nights of the year. Calan Gaeaf marked the start of winter, ushering in a period of cold and darkness. It was also the end of a season of long work under the sun, and as such an opportune time to host grand celebrations to give thanks for all that the land had provided up to this point. *Calan Gaeaf* literally translates to mean 'the calends of/first day of Winter'. The night before Calan Gaeaf was *Nos Galan Gaeaf* (the eve of winter). On our modern Gregorian calendar, this celebration falls on the 1st of November, with *Nos Galan Gaeaf* celebrated on October 31st, lining up with the modern-day Halloween.

And indeed, like the modern Halloween, this was a night of tricks and treats. As with the other two spirit nights, a bonfire was lit on the eve of Calan Gaeaf, but this time with a rather morbid tradition attached to it. In some areas, communities would write their names on a stone and throw it into the fire. There it would be left, until the following day. On Calan Gaeaf day itself they would journey to the location of the bonfire, and they would search the ashes of the pyre for their stone. If they were successful in finding their stone, then the year ahead would be uneventful, and full of luck. However, if their stone had mysteriously vanished in the night, then they took this as an omen that they were certain to die at some point in the next year.

As folks rushed home after an evening of merriment around the bonfire, a warning for those who might dare staying out too late was sung:

> *"Adref, Adref am y cynta,*
> *Hwch Ddu Gwta a gipia'r ola!"*
> - (Jones, 1930)

This verse translates to "Home! Home! Be the first one home! The *Hwch Ddu Gwta* will take the last to get home!". The *Hwch Ddu Gwta* is a folk devil, a spectral black tail-less sow who roams the landscape on the eve of winter, snatching up those who stay out too late in the dark of night. She lurks in the shadows, and children across Wales know to fear her. This isn't just a tradition of the past, even I was raised to fear the *Hwch Ddu Gwta* growing up.

The belief surrounding the *Hwch Ddu Gwta* only furthers the very spirit of Nos Galan Gaeaf. It is a night when all manners of creatures lurk in the shadows. When the spirits of the dead can be spotted at every stile, otherworldly monsters are around every corner, and terrible things can happen if one is not too careful.

Various forms of divination were carried out on this night. From the stone throwing divinatory rite mentioned above, to traditions which call on the participants to walk around a graveyard anywhere from three to nine times in order to gain insight about who would die in the next year, or to conjure a spirit to appear before them.

Folklore stated that the King of the fairies, Gwyn ap Nudd, was also associated with this night. He would fly over Cadair Idris, a mountain located in Eryri, every Nos Galan Gaeaf, preparing to gather the souls of the dead with his hunting hounds, the *Cŵn Annwfn* running at his side (Rudiger, 2021). We might also turn to Deities who deal with magic, liminality, the dead, and the darker aspects of life at this time of year. Cerridwen, Gwydion, Math, and Arawn to name a few.

Druidic Holidays

The most well-known version of the Neopagan 'Wheel of the Year' is not an authentic calendar of ancient Pagan celebrations tied to any particular culture, but instead an eclectic mish-mash of various significant days from a variety of cultures. The one Welsh name for any of the eight festivals on the popular wheel is 'Mabon'. However, it is important to state once again that this is not the name of a Welsh celebration, but instead the name of a Deity who has no ties to the autumn equinox. To read more on that, look to the 'Mabon' section in Part II of this book.

There is, however, another wheel one might come across when exploring modern Paganism, and that is the Druidic wheel of the year. Interestingly, this wheel utilises Welsh names for the four primary celebrations, the solstices and equinoxes. They are as follows:

Alban Eilir – The Spring/Vernal Equinox
Alban Hefin – The Summer Solstice
Alban Elfed – The Autumnal Equinox
Alban Arthan – The Winter Solstice

Where do these names come from? And do they have any rooting in Welsh culture?

These are not traditional names for celebrations that were held in Wales at these times throughout the year. In fact, the earliest these names were likely used for the solstices and equinoxes was in the 19th century. These names originate within the work of Welsh antiquarian and poet Edward Williams, who is better known by his bardic name Iolo Morganwg. Edward Williams was an instrumental figure in the Druidic revival in Wales and has left his mark on Welsh culture as a whole. It is unlikely that Welsh culture would look how it does today if it were not for him. In the same vein, it is unlikely modern Druidry would look the way it does today if it were not for him either.

Considering these names for the equinoxes and solstices are relatively modern, using them is sometimes compared to the use of the term 'Mabon' for the Autumn Equinox. I, however, disagree with that notion. The term 'Mabon' was not only transplanted onto the Autumn Equinox, but it was done so with little to no respect for who Mabon is, nor the culture he is connected with. This Welsh name was placed onto the equinox by someone from outside of Welsh culture, purely for aesthetic reasons. Mabon means nothing in relation to the equinox, without having to twist and contort the story of Mabon ap Modron. Whereas Edward Williams was a Welshman, was very learned in the Welsh literary tradition, and chose the 'Alban' names for these events carefully.

The term 'Alban' within this context means a period of three months, or simply an equinox or solstice. Let's break down the other words at play here too.

Eilir – This word simply means spring, renewal, or regeneration. It denotes a reanimation, or even a return of moisture. As such, 'Alban Arthan' translates to mean 'Period of Regeneration', 'Equinox of Renewal' or simply 'Spring Equinox'.

Hefin – Originating from words associated with the summertime. We see this word appear in the name for the month of June in Welsh (Mehefin) as well as in the word *cyntefin* which means the beginning of summer. Therefore 'Alban Hefin' simply translates to mean 'Period of Summertime' or 'Summer Solstice'.

Elfed – Similar to the words we have already looked at, this word simply translates to mean 'Autumn'. It likely has its origins in words pertaining to mead, apples, and harvests. However, within the context of 'Alban Elfed' it simply means 'Autumnal Equinox'.

Arthan – This is likely the most poetic of the bunch. *Arthan* is the diminutive or juvenile form of the word *Arth,* meaning bear. Therefore 'Alban Arthan' can be translated to mean 'the Solstice of the Bear Cub'. This is likely a reference to Arthur, whom Iolo might have viewed as a representation of the divine child who is born at the winter solstice.

As we see by looking at these words, whilst relatively modern they still carry a simple and effective resonance within Welsh culture. The names make sense, for the most part, and have been part and package of Welsh culture now since the 19th century. Things need not be ancient in order to be authentic, and so if you feel particularly drawn to these names for the seasonal celebrations then by all means, use them.

Chapter 7

Putting It into Practice

All of the information discussed throughout this book so far is nothing without you. You must now seek the Awen, to form a practice that can work with your own personality, and day to day life. A practice that I find works best is one that draws inspiration and information from the past, whilst being rooted in who and what we are today. As we move into Part II of this book, ask yourself how your own personal relationship with the Gods might look? Throughout the previous chapters, and in certain sections beyond, I have attempted to provide crumbs of information pertaining to how I personally incorporate elements of myth, lore, and magic from this cultural stream into my modern-day practice as a Witch today. Perhaps some of those insights might enable you to move forward and pave your own way.

On the Topic of Cultural Appropriation

I am often asked whether it is appropriate for those outside of Welsh culture to embrace the Gods of our landscape, as well as elements of our magical traditions and practices. It is heartwarming that more are now open to the consideration that we need to be more mindful and respectful when approaching cultures that are not our own.

It is my personal belief that the lore and information provided within this book are not part of a closed culture or tradition. Therefore, you do not need to have been born in Wales, speak the Welsh language, nor have Welsh heritage in your ancestral line in order to embrace them. They are open for all to embrace. When Welsh people began settling across the world, they took their songs, their stories, their language, and their culture with them and shared them. I see no reason why it should not be the same today.

However, there is a caveat to this. The culture of Wales, especially when it comes to our native traditions, practices, stories, and language, have long been suppressed and looked down upon. Even today a day does not go by that I do not hear, either in person or online, rather backward and bigoted opinions and statements regarding our culture and language.

It is important that if you have a love for our mythology, magic, and lore that you accept that it has all been shaped by who we are. Our history has made us into who and what we are today, and unfortunately that history can be rather bleak. It was not very long ago that children were punished for speaking their own native language here in Wales. There has long been a movement to attempt to homogenise Britain to fit under the imperial rule and cultural values of England. Our language and culture were long seen as backwards, pointless, and nothing more than a living fossil. And these ideas still persist to this day. I cannot explain how often I come across someone who will loudly and confidently say things such as *"no one even speaks Welsh today, it's a dead language"* or *"There's no point in learning Welsh, most of Wales do not even speak it, it would be better to learn a more useful language like French or Spanish"*.

These attitudes are an echo of centuries of suppression of who we are as a people. And that is part of the story of who we are. It is part of the story of the Gods of this landscape.

My request to those reading this book in landscapes far from Cymru today, is to approach our Gods, our magic, our lore, and our traditions with respect. Neopagan traditions have a history of attempting to homogenise the cultures of the Celtic language speaking countries for decades. We see this specifically within the context of Welsh lore with how our Deities are often just referred to as "Celtic Deities" as opposed to Welsh or Brythonic Deities. We also see a sense of disrespect echoed in the ways that our Deities and stories have long been snatched up, twisted and contorted to such a degree that when compared to their cultural context they are unrecognisable.

Whether it be plucking the name of a Welsh God and attaching it to a holiday which he has no relation to within his original cultural context, or watering down a Welsh Goddess and applying associations to her that have no ties to who she is in her original lore. We see it played out daily.

And so, my advice, is move with respect. Listen to native voices, learn a little of our language, learn about our history, and remind yourself that Welsh culture isn't a thing of the past, it is alive today. We are not some mythical Celtic nation where women with long flowing locks of auburn hair gallop on horseback as fairies and dragons fly around her. We are a modern nation like anywhere else in the world, with our own modern issues and identities. Familiarise yourself with who we truly are, in a nuanced and well-rounded manner. Native Welsh folks like me will thank you for it, and so too will the Gods and spirits of this landscape.

How to Use the Second Part of This Book

As you will come to see, the following pages contain a list of Welsh Deities with short segments detailing who they are within lore, legend, and myth, as well as how they might be interacted with in the modern day. This book should be treated primarily as an index of Deities, and not an in-depth guide. The information provided will hopefully grant you enough detail to go forward and delve deeper if you so wish. Where possible I have provided direction regarding which stories and resources information pertaining to the Deity being focused on might be found. I urge you to seek out those sources in order to further your relationship with these Gods. Further, look to the bibliography at the back of this book as well.

It would not be possible to provide an exhaustive list of all Deities associated with Welsh culture. As this book has illuminated, the topic of Welsh Deities is one that is full of complexity and debate. There will be some Deities featured in this list that will make a few readers scratch their heads and wonder why I have included them. I am sure there will be others who will be wondering where other Deities I might have missed are. Please note that I attempted to discuss as many Deities as I could, but do not move forward expecting this to be a full and complete list of every Deity possible. I don't believe any author could ever achieve such a feat. Our landscape, culture, and mythos are brimming with intriguing entities that are reaching out to us. As such, I apologise if I have missed a Deity you feel incredibly attached to, and please know it was likely not purposeful.

May this book act as a bridge to aid you in connecting with the Deities, spirits, and magic of this landscape I so love.

Part II

Part II

Chapter 8
Deities

Amaethon fab Dôn

An obscure and lesser-known Deity, Amaethon's name only appears once in the prose tales, and that is within the tale of *How Culhwch won Olwen.* Within this story Amaethon seems to be portrayed as a highly skilled farmer, the only agricultural worker who is able to tame wild and rugged land.

This identification of Amaethon as someone with skill in working the land fits well with his name, the word *amaeth* can be literally translated to mean agriculture and is related to words used to describe ploughmen or farmers. With the suffix of *on*, which is an indicator of greatness or divine status Amaethon's name could be poetically translated to mean: The great or divine agriculturalist.

The fact he is in the family of Dôn places him as one of three in this lineage who have a name ending in '-on' and having a connection to skilled crafts. Amaethon is the divine agriculturalist, whereas Gwydion is the divine magician, and Cofannon the divine blacksmith. Magic, smithing, and farming – three skilful crafts both historically and within mythology.

Within modern polytheistic traditions, the house of Dôn is associated with the realm of land, and all three of these skills have an earthly, land-based quality to them. Gwydion's magical power is not described as an Otherworldly power, but one that is rooted in a mastery of words, and also in his relationship to the trees and plants in the landscape around him. Gofannon is a blacksmith, someone who transforms the minerals of the earth into metals and shapes that metal into tools which can be utilised for battle, but also for agricultural needs. And, of course, Amaethon's craft lies in working the land itself. The skills of the Earth.

Beyond the mention of him in *How Culhwch won Olwen* Amaethon's name appears in some of the Taliesin poetry where his relationship with the house of Dôn is again confirmed.

Aranrhod

Also known as Arianrhod. Best known for her role in the fourth branch of the *Mabinogi,* where she is the sister of Gwydion, and niece of Math. After the events of the first half of the fourth branch, Math, the wizard-lord of Gwynedd, requires a new virgin he might rest his feet in the lap of. Aranrhod is suggested, and her virginity is tested. Math places his wand down, and she must step over it. The moment she does she gives birth to a child – Dylan. As she flees, a second "thing" drops out of her, and Gwydion takes this "thing" to his chamber. The "thing" eventually becomes a child. Aranrhod, when presented with the child, scorns him and places three *Tyngedau* (fates) upon him. He shall never have a name, never be able to wield weapons, and never be able to marry a woman of mortal stock. All three of these fates are eventually broken via the magical trickery of her brother Gwydion.

This depiction of Aranrhod often leads people to perceive her as a vicious and cruel woman. I have seen several depictions of her as a sort of caricature of the "wicked step-mother" trope found in other European fairy tales and such. Though, personally, I do not believe she fits this role at all.

Contrastingly, however, Aranrhod has taken an entirely different expression within modern Paganism and Witchcraft. Today you will find several books by Pagan authors who discuss Aranrhod as a beautiful, floaty, ethereal Goddess of the moon and stars. A Goddess of fate, of Witchcraft and magic, or even of reincarnation. But who is Aranrhod within her true cultural context?

Many of the ideas surrounding Aranrhod being a "Goddess of the Moon" stem not from any aspect of lore rooted within Welsh culture, but instead in modern perspectives of how her name might be interpreted. The name, when expressed as 'Arianrhod' is composed of the words *Arian* which translates to mean 'silver', and *rhod* which is an old word meaning 'wheel'. The fact her name can be translated to mean 'The Silver Wheel' has led many to interpret her as a moon Goddess.

However, her name is in actuality more consistently presented within Welsh manuscripts not as Arianrhod, but Aranrhod (Bromwich, 2014). Scholarly modern translations of the *Mabinogi* tend to favour the spelling Aranrhod for her name due to its consistency within the manuscript tradition. If we are to consider this spelling of her name, then the meaning behind it also changes. The suffix of 'rhod' in the name still denotes a wheel, however, *Aran* no longer translates to mean silver. The word *Aran* is usually used to denote the highest point or summit of a mountain or hill in modern Welsh today. It could be translated to essentially mean 'large, humped mound'.

An alternative idea, however, was presented by Welsh scholar Sir Ifor Williams in 1930. *Aran* can also be translated to represented that which holds the wheel in place so that it may spin in motion. An axle. Therefore, an alternate poetic translation of Aranrhod's name might instead be 'The still point at the centre of the turning wheel'. I personally prefer this interpretation of Aranrhod's name, and it grants us a visual of who she is as a Goddess.

She is that which allows events to move. She is the initiatrix, that which keeps the wheels turning. Her power is to direct and turn the wheels surrounding her, she is not a puppet but a puppeteer, pulling the strings.

Beyond her appearance in the fourth branch of the *Mabinogi* Aranrhod also appears in a few Triads and poems. She is depicted in various sources as a beautiful woman, daughter of Dôn according to the fourth branch, and a daughter of Beli Mawr according to the Triads. In the Tallesin poem *Kadeir Kerritucn* (The Chair of Cerridwen) she is described as fairer than the radiance of a sunny day, and she dwells in a court surrounded by a raging river (Haycock, 2007).

Aranrhod is a Goddess of immense transformation, one who will challenge you in order to reveal your true fate. But beyond that she is the still point. She is an inherently transgressive force, in her primary myth she has no connection to any man, she rejects the roles placed upon her due to her gender, and she is powerful and secure in her own being. She can aid us in accepting the parts of ourselves that society by and large wishes for us to be ashamed of. Aranrhod forces you to acknowledge what aspects of your life you are unstable within, and she reminds you to centre yourself, to find your still point at the centre of the ever-turning wheel.

Arawn

King of Annwfn, the Otherworld, in the four branches of the *Mabinogi*. Arawn comes into contact with Pwyll, lord of Dyfed in the South of Wales, at the start of the first branch of the *Mabinogi*. The young and thoughtless mortal lord sends Arawn's hunting hounds away from their recently killed stag so that his own dogs may feast upon the stag's meat. When Pwyll discovers the hunting hounds belong to Arawn, King of Annwfn, he wishes to right his wrong. Pwyll is tasked with helping Arawn to defeat his enemy, Hafgan, who is encroaching upon his territory.

Pwyll completes this task and defeats Hafgan, and by the end of the first branch a relationship develops between Pwyll's kingdom and Arawn's. Arawn sends Pwyll and his descendants' gifts from the Otherworld, including pigs which are said to be Otherworldly creatures in Welsh mythology.

Beyond Arawn's role in the first branch of the *Mabinogi* he does not come up much at all in any other texts or poems. Occasionally in folklore collections he is referenced as the owner and leader of the *Cŵn Annwn*, the Otherworldly hunting hounds. Within their folkloric context they run through the skies gathering the souls of the dead. There are also ghost stories from around the region of Ceredigion in the South-West of Wales which describe ghosts who utter the phrase *"Hir yw'r dydd a hir yw'r nos, a hir yw aros Arawn"* (Long is the day and long is the night, and long is the wait for Arawn).

Among contemporary polytheists, Arawn is often venerated as an Otherworldly Deity – a God who helps us connect with the mysteries and the magic of the Otherworld. This fits well with his role in mythology, as he does act as a bridge between the mortal world and the Otherworld in numerous ways throughout the first branch of the *Mabinogi*. To Pwyll he acts as an initiator and guide, opening his eyes to a world beyond his own and aiding him in travelling into this land. Later, when Pwyll (disguised as Arawn by magic) has completed the task Arawn gave to him, a friendship blossoms between the mortal kingdom of Dyfed, and the Otherworldly kingdom of Annwfn. Arawn is said to send gifts in the form of livestock, food, and treasures to the kingdom of Dyfed, even after Pwyll's death.

In the fourth branch of the *Mabinogi*, we are made aware of the fact that Dyfed is the only kingdom in Wales who have pigs. Pigs, according to Welsh mythology, are Otherworldly fairy creatures. Arawn gifts Pwyll's son, Pryderi, pigs. Gwydion, the wizard from a kingdom in Gwynedd, North Wales, manipulates an entire war by convincing his lord, Math, that it is unfair they are the only ones with pigs.

Arawn may be viewed as a bridge between worlds – he who initiates us into the mysteries of the Otherworld. He asks us to challenge ourselves, to walk with integrity, and to be just in our actions.

Arthur

The legendary King Arthur is a complex figure, and one many might be perplexed to stumble upon in a book on Welsh Deities. Could Arthur be classed as a Welsh God?

It would be easy to believe that everyone reading this book has heard of King Arthur – whether that be through reading the Arthurian tales, watching television series' such as BBC's *Merlin*, or simply in passing. King Arthur is an icon of British mythology. The frustrating paradox with Arthur, however, is that he is often presented as an "English" figure, despite the fact his origins extend into Britain's Brythonic Celtic past.

The King Arthur most people are intimately familiar with today is the one who pulls a sword named Excalibur from an anvil (or stone), has a Queen named Guinevere by his side, and who rules from his castle in a place named Camelot. This Arthur suffers adultery when his wife sleeps with one of his men, Lancelot. Eventually, Arthur is killed by his own nephew during a battle at a place named Camlan. After his death he is taken to the magical Isle of Avalon, where he will sleep until the land is in need of him once again.

The lore behind this romantic and often presented as "English" expression of Arthur comes to us primarily from Sir Thomas Mallory's 15th century *Le Morte D'Arthur* and later English literature. However, Arthur is a figure who has been around far longer than this.

The earliest versions of King Arthur present a Brythonic King, leading his people into battles against the invading Germanic-speaking forces arriving onto the shores of Britain from the continent (Williams, 2021). Invading forces who would, eventually, add to the mixing pot that would become the English. Rather than a symbol of what it means to be English, this was a leader who spoke a Celtic language (the ancestor language of Welsh) and fought tooth and nail to try and protect his native culture, people, and landscape.

Whether or not King Arthur was indeed a real historic King has been a topic of great discussion for centuries. It is impossible to say for certain whether a real King Arthur did exist, primarily due to lack of evidence. The little evidence we do have come from medieval manuscripts such as the 9th century *Historia Brittonum*, the 10th century *Annales Cambriae* and brief references in earlier texts such as the *Gododdin*. In these earliest texts which relate to Arthur, there is no mention of many of the iconic aspects of Arthurian literature today.

If we were to assume that a real King named Arthur ruled in Britain in history, then it is likely he would have been alive between AD 450 and AD 550 (Bromwich, Jarman, and Roberts, 1991). If this is the case, then the historical Arthur would likely have been an early Christian British ruler, battling against the invading Pagan Saxon forces. However, it is important to acknowledge that most recent scholarship shies away from the notion that Arthur was a real King, and the Arthur we know and love today has become a great legend shrouded in mythology, magic, and mystery.

Before any mention of the knights of the round table, Camelot, and Excalibur enter into the literary scene, King Arthur appeared in early Welsh literature as a folkloric entity. In the tale of *How Culhwch won Olwen*,Arthur is Lord of a court named Celli Wig, located in what is today, Cornwall. He has three primary men who ride with him on adventures. These men have preternatural abilities, and together they form a team which could easily be compared to superhero team ups in modern day comic books and films.

Arthur also appears in poetry, such as *Preiddeu Annwfn* (The Spoils of Annwfn) which details a quest into the Otherworld. The Arthur of these early Welsh texts is an adventurous, exciting character. He ventures on great quests and expeditions, he battles against Witches, giants, and hound-headed creatures. An energetic and powerful King. He is quite alien to the later chivalrous, noble King Arthur of French and English literature.

The Arthur of the Welsh is an altogether different Arthur to the King Arthur that is beloved in the popular culture and media of today.

The question, then, is whether we might consider Arthur a Deity or not. Whilst there is no concrete proof which indicates Arthur may be inspired by a pre-Christian God, he has by today become so incredibly iconic and elevated to mythological status that it would be difficult to argue the process of apotheosis has not happened to him. I have met several modern-day Pagans who do view Arthur as a sort-of Deity within their personal practices. Often, they are under no illusion that he has an origin in any ancient Deity but instead accept that his influence on our culture here in Wales (and in Britain as a whole) has transformed him into a great figure worthy of reverence.

Beli Mawr

An ancestral Deity, consort of the Goddess Dôn, patriarch of the House of Dôn. Beli is again a rather shadowy and elusive figure, mentioned only by name in the primary stories many know and love. Today, Beli is venerated as a mighty sky God, a Deity whose domain is the far-reaching heavens above.

The name 'Beli' appears in many of the legendary lineages of Wales, with notable historical and legendary figures tracing their family trees back to a great and powerful entity named Beli. Within our legendary histories the Roman Emperor Maxen was said to have conquered the Island of Britain from a ruler known as Beli ap Manogan, who very likely is one and the same as the mythic figure of Beli Mawr. This is all but confirmed in the story of *Lludd and Llefelys* where the titular characters are introduced to us as the sons of Beli Mawr, son of Manogan.

For many decades scholars have linked Beli Mawr with the Gaulish Deity, Belenos, stating that it is likely Beli's name is cognate with Belenos and his character may carry an echo of a British equivalent to this shining, light-associated Deity. One such scholar who drew links between Beli Mawr and Belenos was Sir Ifor Williams. This provides us with some background as to why many modern-day Polytheists and Pagans venerate Beli Mawr not only as a sky Deity, but a solar Deity.

It is likely Beli's name is etymologically linked with the Welsh word "pelydr" or "pelydrau" meaning "ray" or "rays", relating specifically to light. Whilst the words "Beli" and "pelydr" may not look similar in written form to those who do not speak the Welsh language, they are pronounced incredibly similarly. This only further solidifies the notion of Beli being a solar Deity.

However, it is important to acknowledge that Beli's association with Belenos, and by extension his role as a solar Deity is debated. Scholar John Koch, for instance, argues that there is little to no connection between Beli and Belenos. The notion that Beli is a Welsh or British expression of Belenos is falling out of favour, even among Polytheists. This raises an interesting question, if much of the associations of Beli as a solar and sky God rests on this connection with Belenos, does that mean we are venerating him incorrectly?

Despite arguments against his connection to Belenos, his name is still likely linked to words associated with light, or more specifically rays of light. He may also hold a connection to another Gaulish Deity, Bolgios or Belgius, a Deity associated with thunderous, tempestuous skies.

Within my own personal practice, I venerate Beli as the great sky God, as well as a powerful ancestral figure. Whilst his links to other sky Deities are debated, we cannot ignore the associations that exist beyond supposed connections to ancient Deities. The etymology of his name, and the fact that his descendants within the *Mabinogi* are often associated with celestial bodies and constellations points us towards a Deity who resides in the mighty skies that frame all of our lives.

Bleiddwn

A child born of the union between Gwydion and his brother Gilfaethwy, whom mated in the form of animals during their punishment after the events of the fourth branch of the *Mabinogi*. Each child, three boys, was born as an animal, and was transformed into human form by the Magician-King Math. The children carry a reference to the animal they were born as in their names.

Bleiddwn was born a wolf cub, and as such his name carries the Welsh word for wolf – Blaidd.

Not much is known of the three brothers born of the union between Gwydion and Gilfaethwy beyond their birth and transformation into human form.

Blodeuedd / Blodeuwedd

A woman who is conjured via magic from the flowers of the Oak, Broom, and Meadowsweet. The wizards Math and Gwydion created Blodeuedd to act as a wife for Lleu Llaw Gyffes after his mother, Aranrhod, placed a *tynged* on him which made it impossible for the boy to marry a woman of mortal stock.

In the story Blodeuedd seems incapable of bending to the will of the men around her. She resists conformity, and pursues her heart's desires, even to her own detriment. She falls in love with another man, Gronw Pebr, and with him concocts a plan to kill Lleu Llaw Gyffes so that she may be released from his marriage. Ultimately this leads to Blodeuedd being punished by Gwydion, who transforms her into the most hated of all the birds – an owl.

This entity has two distinct names we see presented in her myth. When she is initially introduced to us, she is Blodeuedd – a name which means "of the flowers". Later, when she is punished and transformed into an owl her name becomes Blodeuwedd – meaning "flower face". This new name echoes her transformation, as the barn owl's face looks very much like a flower. These two names solidify her dual nature, the woman conjured from the wildflowers to the punished creature cursed to venture the land only in darkness. Feared by the creatures of the forest and seen as an omen of misfortune by humans.

Blodeuedd's story has been embraced by progressive thinkers today as a tale of female empowerment. Rather than the story of a sinful woman who commits adultery and is viewed as the antagonist of the story who wishes to murder the hero, she is instead viewed as a woman who will not bow to the whims and wishes of the controlling men around her. Like the flowers she is conjured from, Blodeuedd is wild and untameable. She teaches us an important lesson, that try as we might we will never be able to tame the wild world around us. And perhaps we should not even attempt to.

In many modern polytheistic traditions, she is also venerated as a Goddess of seasonal sovereignty. During the lighter half of the year, when the flowers are in bloom and the sun shines on the lush landscape, we honour her as Blodeuedd – the flower maiden. In the darker half of the year, during the cold and slower times of autumn and winter, we honour her as Blodeuwedd – the owl.

A potent magical ally to call upon when working with plants, herbs, trees, and flowers. Or perhaps when dealing with issues concerning personal sovereignty, freedom, and liberation from predetermined roles placed upon us. Blodeuedd/Blodeuwedd has become one of the most beloved Deities from Welsh tradition today.

Braint

The Welsh equivalent to the Irish Brigid/Brigit/Brig is Ffraid or Braint. Within Christian culture in Wales Sant Ffraid was an Irish nun who sailed over to Wales on a piece of turf and established churches in her name. However, the name Ffraid in another form in Welsh is Braint, and the name Braint is found in the name of a river located on the Isle of Anglesey.

Rivers often hold the names of Goddesses. For example, the river Dee in Welsh is *Afon Dyfrdwy* which translates to essentially mean 'river of the divine waters' or 'river of the water Goddess'. This river alone has an abundance of connections to Goddesses – It is said an ancient Brythonic Goddess named Aerwen was connected to the river, there is a shrine to the Roman Goddess Minerva on the banks of the river in Chester, the river flows into Llyn Tegid, the legendary home of Cerridwen, and there are even some theories that the name *Dyfrdwy* might be related to an ancient river Goddess which has her Welsh reflex in the form of Dôn (Bromwich, 2014). This is but one example of a river holding the name and lore of Goddesses. We also have Hafren/Severn holding the name of Sabrina, among countless other examples.

Some believe that the name Braint holds a memory of an older Goddess, a Goddess related to the ancient Goddess Brigantia (Hughes, 2014).

In an early Welsh poem titled *Gofara Braint* a story is recounted of when the river Braint broke its banks and flooded the landscape in her grief in response to the death of the King at the time, King Cadwallon. This reference to the river reacting to the death of the ruler of the land brings to mind the notion of Kings being married to the land via a sovereignty Goddess. We see this theme play out in the *Mabinogi* – both Pwyll and Manawydan are given the right to rule by marrying Rhiannon, who embodies the sovereignty of the landscape. Perhaps the river flooding was a metaphor for the Goddess grieving the loss of her consort.

Braint is, at present, not a very well-known Goddess and I have yet to come across a single Welsh polytheist who venerates her who does not either come from Anglesey, or who have ties to the Anglesey Druid Order. Having been raised on the island Braint was one of the first Goddesses I personally reached out to, as her river was a constant neighbour in my life. I crossed her on the way to college, or whenever I needed to leave the island. Her river flows directly beside the ancient monument of Bryn Celli Ddu, and so she is present in any rite or working carried out at that location.

Within my own personal practice, and in the tradition of the Anglesey Druid Order, she is a Goddess associated with spring, healing, sacred waters, poetry, and sovereignty. There is a feast in her honour in early February which we refer to as *Gwyl Braint*, but that you might know better as Imbolc or Candlemas. Every year her waters renew the landscape as the world awakens from the slumber of the colder months.

Brân/Bendigeidfran

During the events of the second branch of the *Mabinogi,* Brân is the ruler over the entirety of the Isle of the Mighty, Britain. He is a giant, and no house could ever contain him. An epithet is placed upon him – Brân Fendigaid, or Bendigeidfran, which translates to mean Brân the Blessed. Interestingly, this epithet is only placed upon him within the narrative of the second branch of the *Mabinogi.* Elsewhere in other pieces of lore he is simply referred to as Brân, or Brân fab Llŷr, Brân the son of Llŷr.

Brân's name means crow or corvid, and he is presented as a powerful, noble, and just ruler. He is passionate about ensuring that reparations are paid when a wrong has been committed, and his love for his family is profound. He crosses the sea to save his sister when she is abused.

At the end of the second branch Brân is mortally wounded, and his death is imminent. He commands his men to cut off his head and take it back with them from Ireland over to Britain. His head somehow stays alive even when detached from his body, and he spends many years on a magical island with the survivors of the war which occurs during the story. Eventually, when the enchantment of the magical island wanes, his head is taken to the White Hill, now Tower Hill in London, and is buried. His head, in this place, acts as a magical protection for the island. His power still protecting his landscape after his demise.

Brân guides us to be wise and just leaders. His role as a leader is exemplified in his battle cry during the war in Ireland "A Fo Ben Bid Bont!" (Let he who leads be a bridge!). As a leader Brân does not sit on the sidelines while his men fight for him, nor does he place himself above or before others. He fights alongside them, and even lays himself down across a river so that his men may cross safely. He teaches us that a true leader should be like a bridge…stable, strong, and a force of connection. For us, as modern-day devotees, he asks of us, what do we do in our lives to act as a bridge? To carry his wisdom forward into the world?

Branwen

The most beautiful woman in the world, and also one of the three chief parents, queens, or ancestors of the Island of Britain. Branwen is the sister of the great King Brân the Blessed, and during the events of the second branch of the *Mabinogi* she is wed to the King of Ireland in order to forge a connection and alliance between the two lands.

In some ways Branwen could be perceived as a sovereignty figure, representing the sovereignty of the Isle of the Mighty. Within modern polytheistic spheres she has been given many titles – Goddess of Love, Beauty, Grief, Trauma, Resilience, and more. On a personal level, if I had to reduce Branwen down to one word (a task I am often not fond of doing) I would say Hope.

Throughout the second branch Branwen suffers tremendously. And yet, throughout the majority of the events she keeps hope. The primary place we see this hope take root is when she trains a young starling to take a message across the sea to her brother, in hopes that he might come to her rescue. Her entire hope is resting on the actions of a small, unpredictable bird.

The term "Brân Wen" (white crow/corvid) is still used in some parts of Wales today to denote a rarity, something deeply uncommon. Local Anglesey folklore states that starlings gather in murmuration around the Afon Alaw, where the myth states she dies, as they are descendants of the starling who helped her. They dance in memory of the princess who suffered so greatly. Many can relate to Branwen, and how at the hands of her suffering she took all the blame for the actions of others. Something many women continue to do. It is not surprising then that she is one of the most beloved characters in the *Mabinogi*, and one of the most revered Welsh Goddesses today.

Cerridwen

Goddess of inspiration, skilled witch, the prototypic bard, and distributor of Awen. Cerridwen is well loved and revered the world over today. It is from her cauldron that divine inspiration arises, and the bards sing her praise in hopes that her magic may touch them and their work.

The most well-known story featuring Cerridwen is that which is dubbed *Ystoria Taliesin* and tells the tale of the birth of Taliesin. This story in its entirety is found in its earliest form in the 16th century manuscript dubbed *Elis Gruffudd's Chronicle*. Due to this tale as we have it handed to us being somewhat younger than the manuscript tradition that preserves stories such as those of the four branches of the *Mabinogi*, the tale of Taliesin's birth has been relegated to the realms of "early modern folk tale". There are hints, however, that this tale is far older than the written version we have preserved.

Some of the earliest references to Cerridwen we have in the written record come from a period of the Welsh bardic tradition referred to as the "Gogynfeirdd era" (Hughes, 2021). The *Gogynfeirdd* were bards that were active between the 1100's and the 1300's. The poems of the Gogynfeirdd reference Cerridwen as being an entity associated with the Awen. The best of all bards are privy to the mysteries of the crafts of Cerridwen, and their songs rise from the depths of Cerridwen's cauldron.

We also find reference to Cerridwen and the themes present in the tale of Taliesin's birth in some of the poems in the 14th century *Book of Taliesin*. Certain poems, such as *Mabgyfreu Taliesin* and *Kadeir Kerrituen* name Cerridwen explicitly. Others such as *Angar Kyfundawt* and *Prif Gyuarch Geluyd* reference some of the themes and plotlines featured in the folk tale of Taliesin's birth.

Practically every poem which sings the song of Cerridwen emphasises her association with the Bardic tradition and with the Awen. She is the force which directs Awen into our world, she is described as the blueprint of all bards, that bards can only hope to emulate a fraction of the talent of. The poem *Kadeir Kerrituen* details how if and when poetry shall be judged, hers will always be the best.

With all of this information it is easy to perceive Cerridwen as a Goddess of inspiration, poetry, the Bardic arts. We sing in praise of her in hopes that she might direct the flow of Awen towards us. She is a powerful ally for any creative individual, for from the depths of her cauldron comes the most divine and profound of all inspiration.

In the folk tale of Taliesin's birth, she is also designated as a Witch, a weaver of magic. She is learned in the arts of Witchcraft, Sorcery, and Divination. In her great cauldron she brews a potion of pure Awen which she hopes to give to her son. She is a shapeshifter, capable of changing her form at will.

With this information added to what we already know of Cerridwen she is also tied deeply within Welsh culture today with magic, sorcery, witchcraft, divination. Cerridwen is the prototypic bard, but also the prototypic witch within a Welsh cultural context.

Bards sing her praise, witches look up to her, she is the mother of Awen, and the initiatrix into the mysteries of the magical arts.

Cigfa

Introduced to us in the third branch of the *Mabinogi*, Cigfa is the consort of Pryderi and is left behind with Manawydan when Pryderi and Rhiannon are trapped in Llwyd ap Cilcoed's trap. She, along with her husband Pryderi, goad Manawydan to take action when he seems inactive during the events of the third branch.

Interestingly, one way we could interpret the translation of Cigfa's name is as "the meat place", which in and of itself is rather strange. However, Pryderi's name literally translates to mean anxiety. Therefore, could we interpret "the meat place" to be a reference to the physical body? Which gives us an intriguing premise: Anxiety is married to the body. It is a condition rooted in physicality as opposed to being of the spirit.

Beyond her role in the third branch of the *Mabinogi*, there is not much else that could be said about Cigfa.

Cymidei Cymeinfoll

One of the two original giants who were the guardians of the *Pair Dadeni* (The Cauldron of Rebirth) prior to it coming under the care of Brân. Originating in Ireland alongside her husband Llasar Llaes Gyfnewid, Cymidei was said to have an intriguing ability: She was able to birth fully grown, and fully armed warriors.

Cymidei Cymeinfoll's name translates to mean, in a poetic sense, "she who is heavily pregnant with battle". She is a living cauldron, and like the cauldron she is guardian over, warriors rise from within her ready to face whatever conflict might be before them.

After Matholwch and his men had attempted to murder Cymidei and her husband in an iron house, they sought refuge in Wales and gifted the *Pair Dadeni* to Brân. Once settled in Wales, they populated the landscape with their warriors who had the finest of weapons.

Dôn

An ancestral Deity, matriarch of the family primarily focused on in the fourth branch of the *Mabinogi* comprising of characters such as Math, Gwydion, and Aranrhod. Like other ancestral Deities such as Beli Mawr and Llŷr, Dôn does not appear much in prose tale, but her name is brought up within the context of parentage.

Her name is considered cognate with the Irish Danu (Bromwich, 2014), who unfortunately is also a relatively obscure Goddess about whom many misconceptions abound.

Dôn is revered today primarily as a Goddess who is guardian of the realm of land. She has possible connections with rivers, such as the *Afon Dyfrdwy* (River Dee). Rivers are after all the veins of the landscape, providing nutrients and nourishment for the soil which enables rich crops and plant growth. She is the Mother River, the source of all nourishing waters.

Dôn also has an association with the night sky. In Welsh the constellation of Cassiopeia is referred to as *Llys Dôn* (Dôn's Court), and many members of her family also have starry associations – such as Aranrhod who is associated with the Corona Borealis, or Gwydion who is associated with the Milky Way. This has led many to also view Dôn as an ancestral star Goddess, reminding us that our ancestors are with us always, in the light of the starry skies.

Dylan eil Don

The son of Aranrhod, born during her virginity test in the court of Math. His name refers to the sea and reflects his nature in the fourth branch. Upon being born he almost instantly makes his way to the sea, where he becomes one with the waves.

Not much is known about Dylan beyond a brief mention of his death. He is said to die at the hands of Gofannon, the smith God. It is likely an entire body of myth relating to Dylan has been lost to us.

Within the poetry of Taliesin, the bard recounts how all of the waves of Ireland, Scotland, and Britain weep and are deeply bereaved when Dylan is killed. Emphasising his deep connection with the sea.

As such, despite the lack of lore surrounding him, Dylan is revered today as a sea God and sometimes portrayed as a seal or a merman. These portrayals are, of course, born of relatively modern gnosis concerning him and not any Welsh texts, but are beautiful, nonetheless.

Efnysien

The half brother of Brân, Branwen, and Manawydan. Son of Penarddun and Euroswydd. The two brothers seem to reflect a duality, the second branch of the *Mabinogi* states that whilst one is a peacemaker, the other is a provoker of hostility. Efnysien is the latter.

Capable of causing the most loving of brothers to fight, he who stirs the pot and often makes situations worse. Efnysien is presented as one of the primary antagonists of the second branch. Outraged at the fact his half-sister is married to the Irish King and that no one sought his permission before this happened, he viciously attacks the horses belonged to the Irish during the wedding. This is the motive for all the horrendous things that happen to Branwen in the story, leading to the war which ultimately brings us to the death of Brân, Branwen, and even Efnysien himself.

Whilst we might read the second branch and recoil at Efnysien's actions, it is also a reminder that we carry both Efnysien and his brother Nysien within us. We are capable of keeping peace and also initiating conflict. Efnysien reminds us to take notice of when we are weaving peace, and when we are weaving trouble for ourselves and those around us. Whilst perhaps our actions are not always quite as severe as Efnysien's, we have all been in situations where we likely could have handled things better. Where we allowed our inner troublemaker out.

The duality of Nysien and Efnysien remind us to acknowledge all aspects of our being. Reminding us that we are beings capable of great good, but also great destruction.

Elen Luyddog

A Welsh native tale titled *The Dream of the Macsen Wledig* tells the story of how the Emperor Macsen Wledig (Magnus Maximus) once went hunting, and on this hunt, he laid down his head to sleep for a while. Whilst sleeping he had a dream-vision of a faraway land. In this faraway land was the most beautiful woman he had ever seen.

This woman was more radiant than the sun, dressed in the finest of silks and wearing jewels which amplified her beauty. The emperor fell in love with her and wanted nothing more than to find this woman in the waking realms. He sent his men in search of her, and eventually, many years later, they found her. She was a noble woman from the North of Wales, and her name was Elen.

The story of Elen Luyddog is a fascinating one, it concerns the prophetic visions of a Roman emperor brought forth within the dreaming realms. The story recounts themes of the Roman conquest of Britain, and when the Emperor takes the island of Britain for himself and marries Elen three forts are built for her. Her primary fort was located in the territory of Arfon, near to where the modern town of Caernarfon sits today. The other two forts were located in Caerllion (Caerleon in Gwent) and in Caerfyrddin (Carmarthen in West Wales).

Elen would build roads between the forts of Britain, and these roads would be known as *Ffyrdd Elen Luyddog* (The Roads of Elen of the Hosts).

Within her mythological context Elen is associated with sovereignty. Her marriage to the emperor leads to his acceptance and adoration by the native Britons, as though her hand grants him the right to rule as we see with numerous sovereignty figures. She is also associated with the dreaming, the state of being when we are in deep dreaming. Elen appeared to the emperor like a prophetic vision, as though beckoning him to his destiny. She offers him a sense of direction, pulling him towards his destiny to rule over the land. And finally, she establishes connections between the forts of Britain via her tracks, her roads.

It is these qualities that Elen is usually worked with via a modern polytheistic lens. She is now revered by many as Goddess of direction, she who shows us the many possible paths available to us as we traverse our lives. She is also a beneficial ally to call to when attempting to draw forth visions and prophetic wisdom whilst in the dreaming state.

It is important to note that Elen Luyddog is often conflated with the modern Goddess Elen of the Ways. Whilst both Elen Luyddog and Elen of the Ways share associations with tracks and roads, and it is likely that much of the modern lore pertaining to Elen of the Ways (including her name) might have been inspired by the Welsh Elen, they are still distinct entities. There is no implication within Welsh lore that Elen Luyddog is an antlered Goddess, nor that she has any association with reindeer.

Gilfaethwy

The brother of Gwydion. In the fourth branch of the *Mabinogi* Gilfaethwy falls madly in love, or perhaps lust, with Goewin, his uncle's foot maiden. Math must always rest his feet in the lap of a virgin, and in this instance said virgin is Goewin, unless his kingdom is in conflict. In order for Gilfaethwy to have a chance with Goewin, his brother Gwydion concocts a devious plan to manipulate a conflict between the two kingdoms of Gwynedd and Dyfed. This would lead to Math being able to lift his feet from Goewin's lap, and grant Gilfaethwy a chance to sleep with her.

Their plan works, but Math ultimately discovers the plot. Enraged, he punishes the brothers by transforming them into the mating pairs of various animals. They spend time as a pair of deer, wolves, and a wild boar and sow. Together, in these forms, they mate and produce three children – Hyddwn, Hychddwn, and Bleiddwn.

Goewin

A virgin woman who acts as the foot maiden for the wizard King Math in the fourth branch of the *Mabinogi*. Math has a taboo placed upon him – he must always have his feet resting in the lap of a virgin. The only caveat seems to be that he may remove his feet from a virgin's lap in times of conflict. The maiden he lays his feet in the lap of at the beginning of the fourth branch is Goewin.

Goewin is an interesting figure. She seems to embody the King's connection to the land, acting in a way like a sovereignty figure or Goddess. We may even view her as representing the landscape itself. When Gilfaethwy and Gwydion plot to defile her, they are not only committing an awful violation to one woman, but in turn are also defiling the land itself. On top of this, Math's life is dependent on Goewin being a virgin, and as such to add further insult to injury the two brothers also placed Math's life in jeopardy.

Despite his life being endangered, Math's initial reaction to learning of Gwydion and Gilfaethwy's notorious actions is to ensure the safety and well-being of Goewin. He tends to her needs before moving on to punish the brothers for their actions.

Goewin follows in a tradition of sovereignty figures we come across throughout Welsh lore. A Goddess who provides the ruler with the right to rule. In this instance she is akin to other figures such as Rhiannon and Branwen.

Gofannon

God of smithcraft, the divine blacksmith. Little is known about Gofannon beyond the brief mention of him in the fourth branch of the *Mabinogi,* where it is said that he strikes Dylan Eil Don with a killing blow. His name is comprised of the Welsh word for smithcraft *gof/gofan* coupled with the suffix *on* which denotes divinity. Therefore, he is literally the 'Divine Blacksmith'.

Gofannon is likely cognate with the Gaulish Gobannos, also a God of smithcraft. Place names in Wales such as Abergavenny share an etymological link with the God Gobbanos. Gofannon is linked with the house of Dôn, and alongside others in this lineage, such as Amaethon, the divine agriculturalist, and Gwydion, the divine magician, they give us a trinity of Deities associated with specialised crafts.

Gwenhudwy

Mermaid shepherd of the seas. Gwenhudwy is a shadowy and elusive figure, only mentioned in brief occurrences in poems and folk tales. The earliest literary mention of this figure comes from a sixteenth century poem where the rough waves in the waters between mainland Wales and Bardsey Island are referred to as a troop of the sheep of Gwenhudwy (Jones, 1930).

She is also mentioned in folk tales, such as that of Cantre'r Gwaelod, the legend of a Welsh kingdom now submerged beneath the sea.

Whilst what we do know of Gwenhudwy is sparse, we can still paint a picture of a sea-based entity associated with tempestuous waters, currents and tides. She is a powerful mermaid being who has control over the movements of the water. The waves are her flock of sheep, and every ninth wave, the tallest waves of all, are her rams. She steers and directs her waves, and knows when the wind and waves may become stormy.

Within my own practice I have adopted Gwenhudwy as a Goddess of the waves, directrix of the currents, and bringer of sea storms. Having grown up on the coast, and immersed in Welsh myth and lore, she has long intrigued me. I reached out to her from a very young age and sensed her power along the coastal paths that were my childhood playgrounds.

Mermaid Goddess of the tempestuous seas, shepherd of the waves, directrix of currents, keeper of the tides.

Gwenhwyfar

Gwenhwyfar is the Welsh equivalent of Guinevere, the consort of King Arthur. The earliest literary mention of Gwenhwyfar can be found in Geoffrey of Monmouth's *Historia Regum Britanniae* in the 12th century. In Geoffrey's writings her name is spelled *Guenhuuera,* and she is introduced to us as a descendant of a noble Roman family. We are also told that she was raised in the household of a great Duke – Cador.

Gwenhwyfar is mentioned in the Triads, most notably in Triad number 56 which lists three different Gwenhwyfar's, all of which were betrothed to Arthur.

"Arthur's Three Great Queens:

- *Gwenhwyfar, Daughter of Cywryd Gwent*
- *Gwenhwyfar, Daughter of Gwythyr son of Greidiawl*
- *Gwenhwyfar, Daughter of Gogfran the Giant"*

- (Bromwich, 2014)

There has been much discussion as to why there are three Gwenhwyfar's mentioned in this triad. Did Arthur truly take three wives with the same name? Or are all three mentioned here different epithets or reflexes of the same entity? Within Goddess-focused traditions of Neo-Paganism this has led to many seeing her as a complex, triplistic Goddess.

Her name is incredibly interesting. The first part "Gwen" can be translated to mean white, fair, or blessed. The second part "hwyfar" is somewhat more mysterious. This word seems to be cognate with an Irish word *siabair* which denotes a phantom, a spirit, or even a fairy. Some possible translations of her name, then, is fair phantom, or white fairy. Rachel Bromwich in *Trioedd Ynys Prydein* notes that her name is cognate with Queen Medb's daughter in the Irish Ulster epics, Findabair.

Consort to Arthur, regal and noble, daughter of a giant, fair or white spirit. The scattered sources relating to Gwenhwyfar paint a picture of a complex entity in our lore. Many venerate Gwenhwyfar today as a sovereignty figure.

Gwydion

An often troublesome and problematic magician, Gwydion is best known for his role in the fourth branch of the *Mabinogi*. In this branch he starts a war purely to help his brother have a chance with the woman he has fallen for. Gwydion is reckless and dangerous, jumping into situations with little to no forethought. He seemingly lacks any principles, and is the polar opposite to his uncle, Math.

Gwydion is part of the house of Dôn, and as such he is related to Math, Aranrhod, Lleu Llaw Gyffes, and even according to some sources Gofannon and Amaethon. Whilst flawed and reckless, Gwydion also showcases a mastery over magic. A skilled magician, he is a master of his craft in the same way that Gofannon and Amaethon are masters of theirs.

Gwydion's name is somewhat difficult to fully decipher. The most likely meaning behind is name is that it somehow relates to words such as *gwŷdd,* which denotes knowledge, and sciences. The word for 'to know' in Welsh is *gwybod* and the word we use to denote science is *gwyddoniaeth,* both have that *gwy/gwyd-* at the beginning similar to Gwydion's name. However, the word *gwŷdd* also holds associations with trees and forests. This fact might be pertinent as we have evidence of Gwydion in relation to trees in Welsh poetry as well.

Gwydion is featured in the poem *Kat Godeu*, where via his mastery of words and his connection to the land which surrounds him, he conjures an army out of the trees of the forest. He literally calls the trees to action, and as such many modern-day polytheists refer to him as the caller of trees.

When looking at Gwydion via a modern polytheistic lens we might see him as a warning. He is what one might become if we succumb to reckless and thoughtless actions via our magical acts. He is the rash and chaotic magician, who dives into situations wand first. He teaches us that before turning to magic we should have the restraint and patience to consider our actions first, and carefully concoct a plan to fix situations.

Gwyn ap Nudd

A fierce and terrifying warrior, connected to King Arthur and his men, and a flamboyant fairy king. Gwyn ap Nudd seems to take a variety of expressions throughout Welsh lore. Acknowledged by many modern-day Pagans, polytheists, and magical practitioners as a psychopomp, guardian of the mound who keeps the gates between our world and the Otherworld, a King of Fairies, a God of liminality and transition.

The earliest appearance of Gwyn ap Nudd can be traced back to the *Black Book of Carmarthen*. In a poem titled *The Dialogue Between Gwyn ap Nudd and Gwyddno Garanhir* Gwyn appears as a fearsome character striding onto a battlefield after the fighting has come to an end. Gwyn laments the loss of fallen men, and recounts how he has been present at many battles over his lifetime and has witnessed countless deaths. Ravens flock around Gwyn, and the dialogue that takes place between him and Gwyddno Garanhir has led to various Pagan authors to perceive him as a psychopomp, a being who leads the souls of the dead to the afterlife (Hughes, 2014).

Gwyn ap Nudd also appears in the story of *How Culhwch won Olwen*. This tale grants us more information about Gwyn. He is described as having the very spirit of all of the "demons of Annwn" (Davies, 2007) placed within him. Gwyn is essentially presented here as a protector or gatekeeper who keeps the chaotic and troublesome forces of the Otherworld away from our own world. Gwyn rides upon the back of a great stallion named *Du y Moroedd* (the Black of the Seas) who has the ability to gallop across the waves of the sea.

It is in this story that we learn of the constant battle which takes place between Gwyn ap Nudd and another character named Gwythyr son of Greidol. Both Gwyn and Gwythyr long for the hand of a maiden named Creiddylad, and a great conflict arises between Gwyn's men and Gwythyr's. Eventually Gwyn and Gwythyr are fated to forever fight for the hand of Creiddylad. They shall battle every May Day for her hand, and the battle shall take place annually for all of time. Only at the end of all of time shall the victor be granted the hand of Creiddylad.

Gwyn would captivate Welsh audiences throughout the ages, and his character would adapt to suit countless stories. In *Buchedd Collen*, the legendary account of the life of St. Collen, Gwyn is presented as a flamboyant fairy King sat upon a golden throne, who like a sly devil, attempts to entice the monk to feast with him and his fairy court. Collen throws holy water over Gwyn and his court, causing them to vanish. In this tale Gwyn is associated with Glastonbury tor, his court sits upon the top of the tor, invisible at most times.

Gwyn's name can be translated to mean the colour 'white', but also holds associations and connotations of something blessed. The 'ap Nudd' portion of his name simply describe who he is the son of. He is son of Nudd, a character in Welsh lore who is believed cognate to an ancient Deity, Nodens. The word

Nudd can be translated to mean 'mist', and therefore Gwyn's name could be perceived as being 'The Blessed son of Mist'.

There is evidence that Gwyn ap Nudd was invoked in petitionary prayers by soothsayers and magical practitioners in the 14th century (Lindahl, McNamara, and Lindow, 2002). Showcasing that Gwyn ap Nudd has long been a folkloric figure prominent in the folk beliefs of various regions of Wales.

Hafren/Sabrina

Goddess of the *Afon Hafren,* the River Severn, the longest river in Britain. Hafren in Welsh, Sabrina in English. Sabrina's inclusion on this list may be somewhat controversial due to the fact that many might see her as an "English" Goddess, however, it is important to acknowledge that the Severn straddles both countries, and her source is located in the slopes of Pumlumon, in Wales. Her nature therefore defies these national identities, and as such she belongs to both England and Wales today. There are a handful of stories relating to who exactly Hafren is, and where she comes from.

The earliest known literary mention of the Goddess Hafren's origin comes to us from the works of Geoffrey of Monmouth. In Geoffrey's writings Hafren is the daughter of Locrinus, a legendary ruler of England, and a Germanic princess Estrildus. The union of Locrinus and Estrildus was somewhat adulterous, as Locrinus was promised to marry another, a woman named Gwendolen. When Locrinus casts Gwendolen aside in favour of Estrildus, Gwendolen orchestrated the death of Locrinus, and in her rage also ordered the drowning of both Estrildus and Hafren. However, upon her death, Hafren became one with the river, and transformed into a watery Deity who would forever be beloved by those who lived along her waters.

A later Welsh folk tale speaks of Hafren's more elemental, nature-based qualities. In this version she is one of three sisters – Hafren, Gwy, and Rheidol. The three sisters represent the rivers – Severn, Wye, and Rheidol. They are daughters of Pumlumon, and once born they journey towards the sea in their own style. Gwy journeys through the most delightful of natural sights on her journey, Rheidol rushes to the sea as quickly as possible, but Hafren chooses to journey through all of the haunts of man, through cities, towns, and villages. She is said to be particularly fond of Shrewsbury, so much so that she almost carved the town into an island. If you look up Shrewsbury on a map today, you will see how the river wraps around it like a serpent.

Hafren can be viewed in a multitude of ways as a Deity today. She is a guardian of her river, a wild watery spirit, but also a cultural entity who expresses the complexities of her landscape. And whilst she is likely most beloved and venerated by those who dwell beside her waters, the fact she is a Goddess of a body of water, and all waters across the world are connected, means that she cannot be completely contained or restricted.

Hychddwn

A child born of the union between Gwydion and his brother Gilfaethwy, who mated in the form of animals during their punishment after the events of the fourth branch of the *Mabinogi*. Each child, three boys, was born as an animal, and was transformed into human form by the Magician-King Math. The children carry a reference to the animal they were born as in their names.

Hychddwn was born as a piglet, and as such his name carries the word for a sow or a pig – Hych/Hwch.

Not much is known of the three brothers born of the union between Gwydion and Gilfaethwy beyond their birth, given names, and transformation into human form.

Hyddwn

Another child born of the union between Gwydion and his brother Gilfaethwy, who mated in the form of animals during their punishment after the events of the fourth branch of the *Mabinogi*. Each child, three boys, was born as an animal, and was transformed into human form by the Magician-King Math. The children carry a reference to the animal they were born as in their names.

Hyddwn was born as a fawn and therefore carries the word for a stag or hart in his name – Hydd.

Llasar Llaes Gyfnewid

One of two giants who were the original guardians of the *Pair Dadeni* (The Cauldron of Rebirth). Read the above section on Cymidei Cymeinfoll for more information. Llasar's name could potentially translate to mean either ever-changing warrior, or ever-changing flame. Llasar's giant wife, Cymidei Cymeinfoll, acts as a living or personified cauldron of rebirth. She has the ability to birth fully formed, fully armed warriors. Whereas Llasar seems to have associations with weapons, or more specifically shields.

Together they form a pairing which seem to reflect the very power of the cauldron they once were keepers of. Cymidei acts as the vessel, whilst Llasar represents the fuel which aids the cauldron to reach a boiling point. Together creating unstoppable, supernatural warriors. After handing the cauldron over to Brân upon their arrival into Wales from Ireland, Llasar and Cymidei travel around the country populating the land with their exceptional warriors.

Lleu Llaw Gyffes

The son of Aranrhod, born during her virginity test in Math's court. Although, originally, he is but a *pethan*, a 'thing' which drops out of Aranrhod's body, his uncle, Gwydion, picks up this 'thing' and incubates it in a magical chest at the end of his bed. Eventually the 'thing' becomes a boy with shining gold hair.

When Aranrhod becomes aware of his existence she places three *tyngedau* – taboos or fates – upon him. He shall never have a name, shall never carry weapons, and will never be able to marry a woman of mortal stock. Via trickery and magic Gwydion and the boy manage to break these *tyngedau*. He is named Lleu Llaw Gyffes, meaning 'Light of Skilful Hand', he is given weapons by Aranrhod herself, and Gwydion, with the help of Math, conjures a woman out of flowers for him to marry.

Lleu is viewed today as a God of light. His name literally translates to mean light or brightness and can be seen in modern Welsh words such as *goleuni* (light) or *lleuad* (moon). He is the radiant, splendorous warrior God. In the tradition of the Anglesey Druid Order he is called to during the winter solstice, when we ask that the light returns. Gwydion called Lleu down from an otherworldly tree after Blodeuedd and Gronw attempted to kill him, and in keeping with that notion the Druids sing Lleu, and by extension the rays of the summer sunshine, back to us at that transitional, liminal time between the light and dark half of the year.

Lludd/Nudd

In the story of *Lludd and Llefelys* Lludd is the eldest son of Beli Mawr ap Manogan, the ruler of Britain. Upon Beli's death, Lludd inherits the rule of the island. The tale depicts how Lludd re-fortifies the city of London, which is apparently named after him (the Welsh name for London is Llundain, which according to this tale comes from Caer Lludd). Later he deals with three oppressions or plagues which threaten the Island of Britain.

The first plague is an invading force known as the *Coraniaid*, the second is a terrible screech caused by two dragons fighting, and the third is the disappearance of much needed provisions and stocks, which turns out to be the works of a wicked magician. All three of these problems are solved by Lludd, with help from his brother Llefelys.

Interestingly this story references the red dragon of Wales. The terrifying screech which can be heard echoing throughout the land every May Day turns out to be the sound of two dragons fighting. One dragon is red, whilst the other is white. The screech is so terrible and loud that it causes all the pregnant women in the land to miscarry. Eventually Lludd manages to capture the dragons, as they transform into two little pigs. Lludd captures the dragons-turned-pigs by getting them to drink mead, and in their drunken state he wraps them up in a silk sheet and buries them in a vault atop Dinas Emrys. Yes, it is a rather wild and strange story, and a very entertaining one too, do read the tale in its entirety.

We see the name Lludd appear elsewhere in Welsh texts under the epithet Lludd Llaw Eraint, which translates to be Lludd of the Silver Hand. Under this epithet Lludd is cognate with the Irish Nuada Airgedlámh.

Lludd is complex as his identity seems deeply connected with a variety of names from other cultures and traditions. It is likely his name was originally Nudd, which links him with an older Romano-British Deity, Nodons or Nodens. Nodens had a temple located near the River Severn in Gloucestershire. Based on the imagery found on mosaics at the temple in Lydney, we can ascertain that Nodens had an association with the sea and possibly fishing. It is feasible that his name, within Welsh literary tradition, would become Nudd, and due to a fondness for alliteration would later transform into Lludd to fit with both the epithet of Lludd Llaw Eraint, and the title of the story *Lludd a Llefelys* (Bromwich, 2014).

With this in mind, Lludd then, under the name Nudd, is also connected to Gwyn ap Nudd. The 'ap Nudd' in Gwyn's name means son of Nudd. Gwyn has associations with the sea. For example, in Culhwch and Olwen it is said that Gwyn ap Nudd can ride upon a horse which has the ability to gallop over the waves of the sea.

Here we have a complex and often perplexing enigma. A character who is linked with a pre-Christian British Deity associated with the sea, who in literary tradition is viewed as a ruler of Britain and onomastic origin of the city of London. His lore is tangled in stories relating to dragons and foreign invaders, and his name carries a heavy history loaded with cognate reflexes and hints at older traditions.

His brother Llefelys is likely cognate with Lugos, Lugh, and even Lleu Llaw Gyffes. There is certainly a lot to unpack here, and unfortunately no room to do so here. To read more I suggest looking to sources such as Rachel Bromwich's *Trioedd Ynys Prydein* and Sioned Davies' translation of *The Mabinogion*.

Llŷr

Llŷr's name is familiar to any who have read the four branches of the *Mabinogi*, despite the fact he is merely mentioned by name and makes no appearance in the stories themselves. He appears within the context of the *Mabinogi* as an ancestral figure, the father of some of the most prominent characters of the second and third branches. He is the father of Branwen, Brân, and Manawydan. His household is one of the noble households of the Island of the Mighty.

The name Llŷr shares an etymological root with the word 'Llifo' in Welsh, which translates to mean *flow*, as in the *flow* of water. In many pieces of poetry from the medieval period, bards would use the word *Llyrion* to denote the seas. His name clearly expresses characteristics which point us towards the sea and waters.

The name Llŷr also appears in the Triads under a variety of epithets. One of these epithets gifts us yet another association with the sea, Llŷr Marini. This is an interesting name as it includes two different words which denote 'seas' in two different languages. Llŷr, of course, coming from the Welsh or Brythonic expression for the seas, and *Marini*, a Latin word for the sea as well, or more specifically 'of the sea'. Together they could be translated into English to mean "The Sea of the Seas".

Another epithet we come across in the Triads in Llŷr Luyddog, meaning Llŷr of the Hosts. He is also one of three exalted prisoners of the Island of Britain, having been kept prisoner by Euroswydd, the father of Brân, Branwen, and Manawydan's half-siblings Nisien and Efnysien. The Triads hint to there being a greater body of lore associated with Llŷr at some point, though today we have but scattered fragments of said lore.

In modern Pagan and Polytheistic traditions and practices, Llŷr is often revered as a God of the Seas. He and his family hold the power of the sovereignty of Brythonic Britain, and as a house of the sea also remind us of our visceral connections to all things. All land masses on Earth touch the sea at some point, and the waters of our world are all the same water. Cycling in a hydrological cycle where the same water is recycled over and over again. It is the mysteries of the oceans which Llŷr and his household express in their divine natures. The sea is also often expressed in Welsh myth and lore as a connection between our world and the Otherworld – another reminder of just how interconnected we are to the many forces of our reality, both seen and unseen.

Llŷr and his children are the bridges between peoples, worlds, and perceptions.

Mabon

The word 'mab' is used even today in modern Welsh to denote 'son', and that is precisely what the *Mab* in Mabon also denotes. The suffix of *on* signifies either 'great' or 'divine'. As such, Mabon's name can be translated to mean Great or Divine Son.

The name Mabon is primarily recognisable to most today as the character of Mabon ap Modron from Welsh mythology. The tale he is best known for is likely *How Culhwch Won Olwen*, an epic piece of prose which features King Arthur, giants, witches, superpowered individuals, ancient animals, a magical wild boar with highly sought after hair accessories, and dashing heroes fighting for the hand of beautiful maidens.

In this tale the hero Culhwch wishes to marry a maiden named Olwen, and to do so he seeks the approval of her father, Ysbaddaden, who also happens to be the chief giant in all of Britain. Ysbaddaden agrees to the union, under the condition that Culhwch can accomplish a set of seemingly impossible tasks. One of these tasks requires them to find special hairdressing equipment which are the only tools capable of taming the giant's wild, unruly hair and beard. These tools are tucked behind the ears of the *Twrch Trwyth* a wild and magical boar who roams around Britain, Ireland, and even parts of Northern France. The only creature capable of tracking down the boar is a dog named Drudwyn, and the only person capable of handling Drudwyn is a man named Mabon ap Modron.

Unfortunately for Culhwch, however, Mabon was stolen away from his mother, Modron, at only three days old. Not a soul in the land knows the whereabouts of Mabon. King Arthur, who is helping Culhwch throughout his venture, sends some of his men in search of Mabon. One of these men is named Gwrhyr, and he has a very special ability – he can speak all languages known to man and beast. This proves useful as the band realise the only beings that may know Mabon's whereabouts are the Ancients of the World, animals who are said to be older than all other creatures.

They seek out the Ancients of the World, and none save the most ancient of all, the Salmon of Llyn Llyw, know anything of Mabon. The salmon reveals to them that Mabon is kept prisoner in the most dreadful place of all – Gloucester. He carries two of Arthur's men, Cai and Bedwyr, on his back towards the prison he is kept in. There they find Mabon and release him so that he may aid in Culhwch's quest.

Mabon's name may be recognisable to Pagans and Witches today as it appears on depictions of the "Wheel of the Year", the calendar of festivals and observances among modern Pagans. It may be a shock to hear, but the name Mabon is not an ancient name for the Autumn Equinox as the Wheel of the Year might lead some to believe. And in fact, the name Mabon was never used in relation to the Autumn Equinox prior to the 1970's. What is even more baffling is that Mabon in his original cultural context also has nothing whatsoever to do with the Autumn Equinox. So then, why does his name appear on the Wheel of the Year?

The origin of the name 'Mabon' in this context can be traced to a California-based Wiccan named Aidan Kelly. In 2017 Kelly wrote an article for the religious blog site *Patheos* detailing his reasons for naming the Autumn Equinox Mabon. Kelly was also the first person to name the Spring Equinox 'Ostara', and the Summer Solstice 'Litha', though we will not delve into that here.

Kelly explains that he was offended by the lack of aesthetic balance in illustrations of the Wheel of the Year. The fact the calendar which Pagans followed included names such as Samhain, Beltane, and Yule…which were lovely. But then we had such scientific names such as 'Autumn Equinox' and 'Vernal Equinox'. And so, he went on the search for better names for these times of year. On the Autumn Equinox he initially searched for a name from the Anglo-Saxon calendar but failed. And so, he turned his eyes to the myth of Kore from Greek mythology. He concluded that the Celtic or British equivalent to the Persephone myth was the story of Mabon. And that was that the name Mabon was slapped onto the Wheel and has since clearly caught on as it is impossible to find a version of the Wheel of the Year today which does not label the Autumnal Equinox as 'Mabon'.

The issue, however, is that the story of Kore/Persephone and the story of Mabon have little to no similarity at all, beyond the fact that it is about a child stolen from their mother. In writing his explanation for this naming Kelly also proved time and time again that he had very little grasp of the source material he was drawing from. In his article he explains how the story of Mabon is about a boy who is spirited away to the "underworld" and is ultimately rescued by the wizard Gwydion. None of this happens at all. Mabon is not stolen away into the Otherworld but is instead taken at three days old and kept as prisoner for what is assumed to be centuries in Caer Loyw, modern day Gloucester in England. Gwydion does not rescue him from this place, Cai and Bedwyr do. And in fact, Gwydion plays no role in this story whatsoever.

Many Welsh-speaking Pagans today have a strong dislike of Mabon's name being attached to the Autumn Equinox in this manner. It was done with little to no respect for the culture from which Mabon originates and was done due to a very misguided and misconstrued understanding of the source material as well. To make matters worse many Pagans who refer to the Autumn Equinox as 'Mabon' have no idea who Mabon ap Modron is, that he is a Welsh God, nor do they know how to pronounce his name correctly (it is Mah-bon, not May-bon. The 'a' in Mabon is pronounced like the 'a' in English words such as 'Map', 'Cab', or 'Cat' and not as in 'Hay' or 'Tray').

Mabon within his original context is associated with hunting, he can handle the hunting hound Drudwyn, who is able to track down the mystical boar, the Twrch Trwyth. He is an ancient prisoner, only the most ancient animals in the world know of his whereabouts, which seems to imply he has been imprisoned for generations. He is the son of Modron, whose name means great or divine mother. Modron has associations with the Otherworld, and so it is possible Mabon has similar links.

Beyond his specifically Welsh context it is believed that Mabon is also cognate with an ancient Deity worshipped in Britain and Gaul named Maponos. The God Maponos is associated with healing and was viewed as cognate with Apollo by Romans located in Gaul.

I believe that Mabon is far more interesting when viewed within his cultural context and links with reflexes in other cultures as well, rather than merely as being associated with the Wheel of the Year.

Manawydan

A son of Llŷr, brother to Brân and Branwen, one of the golden shoemakers of the Island of Britain. Manawydan is first introduced to us during the events of the second branch of the *Mabinogi*, though it is in the third branch we truly get to know him intimately.

Manawydan is one of the seven survivors of the tragic events which occurred in the second branch. He journeys with Brân and the other survivors to Ynys Gwales and later journeyed to London in order to bury his brother's head at the White Hill. After this, he journeys to the kingdom of Dyfed with Pryderi where he marries Rhiannon.

He is a patient, wise, and incredibly perceptive man. Manawydan seems to know things and see things that others cannot. For example, when the seven survivors are taking refuge on the island of Gwales, he knows that the otherworldly paradise the island provides will all be taken away if a particular door were to be opened. He is not quick to action, which many of his peers criticise him for, but he is prudent and patient instead. In the third branch Pryderi often throws himself into situations which then lead him into trouble, whereas Manawydan is often the first to advise caution.

His name may provide us with an insight into his nature. Whilst his name is likely cognate with the Irish Manannán mac Lir, some scholars have also theorised his name might be linked to the word *mynawyd* which translates to mean an awl (Sims-Williams, 2011). An awl is a device that can pierce through leather, and this is interesting as shoemaking, a craft which requires the use of an awl, is a craft Manawydan is associated with. An awl is that which pierces through material and allows us to take that raw material and transform it into something new. Perhaps this is exactly the quality Manawydan excels in, seeing things from a different angle. Or perhaps seeing something for what it truly is.

Manawydan is a man who is cautious and calculated as opposed to fierce and quick to action. He is prudent, wise, and perceptive. Within magical and spiritual practice Manawydan is a potent ally to call upon when clarity, patience, and wisdom is needed. When we need a new perspective on a situation, or when the same old methods we tend to apply seem to bring about no results.

Math fab Mathonwy

The wise, cautious, and just Wizard-King of the *Mabinogi*. Great Druid, powerful magician, and teacher of magic. The primary source most will know Math from is the fourth branch of the *Mabinogi*, where he is introduced as the Lord of Gwynedd. In this branch Math is also identified as a great magician, and where his nephew Gwydion is often reckless with his magic, Math is cautious and prudent.

Math has a *tynged* (a fate or taboo) placed upon him, he cannot live lest his feet rest within the lap of a virgin. The only instance he was able to lift his feet from the lap of a virgin was if his kingdom was in turmoil or conflict. The maiden he chooses to be with him at the beginning of the fourth branch is named Goewin.

Throughout Welsh lore Math is stated to have an abundance of magical qualities. One particular ability he has is to hear all things. If a whisper is caught upon the wind, it will surely be carried to the ears of Math. Outside of the *Mabinogi*, the Triads refer to Math as one of the three most notable and powerful magicians of the

Island of Britain, alongside Uther Pendragon and Rhudlwm the Dwarf (Bromwich, 2014). Gwydion learnt the art of magic and enchantment from Math, making him a mentor and teacher as well.

Math's name is difficult to decipher. It is likely this name made its way into the Welsh tradition from an older, pre-Christian Deity. We find cognate names from both Gaul and early Ireland. In Irish lore, specifically in the *Lebor Gabála,* the Druid of the Tuatha Dé Dannan is named Math Mac Umóir. The Math of Welsh tradition and the Irish Math share many similarities, both being highly respected leaders deeply associated with magical or spiritual abilities.

With a wave of his magic wand, Math can cause all manners of magics and marvels. He transforms not only the image of individuals to look like someone or something else, but he can change them at their very core or soul. Alongside Gwydion he creates a woman out of the flowers of the forest. Throughout these great magical acts, he employs a sense of caution, consideration, and wisdom.

As such, Math is primarily venerated today as a God of magic. He is the great Druid leader, magician-God, he who teaches us the art of magic and the wisdom to practice that art with great consideration and care. He is also associated with justice, truth, and the keeping of tradition.

Modron

Modron is the mother of Mabon in Welsh mythology. Her name can be translated to mean 'The Great Mother' or 'The Divine Mother'. Modron does not appear in the primary myths we usually turn to as a fully-fledged character, more so she is only mentioned in reference to Mabon. However, hints of a greater body of lore concerning Modron abound.

She is mentioned in the Triads and is said to be the daughter of an Otherworldly King named Afallach, who appears throughout Welsh literature as the son of Beli Mawr, and as part of the genealogies of various important figures throughout Welsh and British history (Bromwich, 2014). The name for the land which King Arthur was taken after his fatal wounds is originally believed to have been Afallach, and therefore this may be the earlier form of what is now known as Avalon (Stephens, 1986).

Modron is also said to be the consort of Urien of Rheged, a King of *Yr Hen Ogledd* (The Old North). She bore him two children, Owain and Morfudd. Peniarth Manuscript 147 features a story which details that Urien and Modron met at a ford where she was washing, and that they had sex in this place and afterwards Modron reveals that she is the daughter of the King of Annwfn.

Modron is considered cognate or a Welsh reflex of the continental Goddess Matrona, a Goddess of the River Marne in France. This mirrors the way in which Mabon is considered connected to the continental Maponos. Similarly, some have drawn parallels between Modron and Rhiannon. Both are great mothers who have their child snatched away. Their child is imprisoned and eventually released.

Among modern polytheists Modron is perceived as a 'Great Mother' Goddess. Many turn to Modron to aid them in connecting to the cycles of life, the seasons, and to deepen their connection to the land beneath their feet.

Myrddin/Merlin/Emrys

Merlin is a figure well known and beloved across the world. In many ways the prototypic wizard, setting the blueprint for how wizards are presented in page and on screen for centuries to follow. Despite how well-known Merlin is, however, many do not realise his origins have a link to the Brythonic and Welsh aspects of British history.

The name we know him under today, Merlin, comes from the work of Geoffrey of Monmouth in the 12th century (Williams,

2021). In his work Merlin is known as Merlinus Ambrosius. The 'Ambrosius' aspect of his name is believed to have derived from the Welsh figure Emrys, whom Geoffrey drew inspiration from in his formation of Merlinus. Emrys is a young, fatherless boy from a story in the 9th century text the *Historia Brittonum* who was originally intended to be a child sacrifice in order to appease the land, but who ultimately revealed himself to be a prophet. King Vortigern attempted to build a castle in an area of North Wales, but the walls of the castle consistently kept falling down overnight. His advisors told him to reverse his fate he must sacrifice a child, but when the child was brought before him the young boy laughed and stated Vortigern's advisors knew nothing. He revealed to the King that beneath the land where the castle was set to be built were two dragons, one red and one white. These dragons were constantly battling, and that is what brought the castle walls tumbling down night after night.

The two dragons represented a prophecy which related to the struggles of the native Britons in this era. The red dragon, who appeared weaker and smaller, represented the native Britons, the ancestors of the Welsh. The white dragon, who appeared larger and stronger, represented the invading forces. Despite the difference in size and strength, and the fact the red dragon seemed on the verge of defeat countless times, the red dragon persisted and continued to fight with ferocity. This illustrated the enduring strength of the native Britons. As such, this story has become the legendary origin story of the Welsh flag today.

Another figure which Geoffrey of Monmouth drew inspiration from for his depiction of Merlin was Myrddin Wyllt (Wild Myrddin). Myrddin was a warrior from the "old north" (a region located in what is today the southernmost regions of Scotland and Northernmost regions of England but was once home to Brythonic speaking peoples). He had fought in a terrible battle in which he witnessed the slaying of many of his fellow warriors and even his Lord, Gwenddolen (Bromwich, 2014).

In response to the terrors he witnessed, Myrddin lost all of his reason and sanity, and so he fled to live a wild, untethered life in the Caledonian forest. Here he would reside as a wild and frantic bard and prophet.

The Merlin of later Arthurian lore is an amalgamation of all of these figures and more. Whilst the Merlin of modern pop culture is a wise and helpful wizard, the figures who inspired such a figure were connected to the bardic arts and the art of prophecy.

Many regions claim Merlin as their own, but the truth of the matter is he really gets around! The boy-prophet Emrys' story takes place in a place known today as Dinas Emrys in Gwynedd, North Wales. Myrddin Wyllt's stories take place in the regions of the Old North, in what is today, Cumbria, Northern England, and Southern Scotland, as well as later, of course, the Caledonian forest. Other Welsh poems and texts describe how Merlin rests on Bardssey Island off the coast of Wales, there he sleeps in a glass house and guards the 13 treasures of Britain. The Merlin of Geoffrey of Monmouth's work is connected to Caerfyrddin (Carmarthen) in the South of Wales. Later lore would associate Merlin with the North of France, Tintagel in Cornwall, and many other locations.

There are also various links between Merlin and Taliesin, including the implication that both Taliesin and Merlin are of the same prophetic spirit, incarnated into different forms (Hughes, 2021).

Merlin represents a spirit which seems present in every generation. He is the prototypic wizard, the archetypal mentor, the inspiring force. He reminds us to seek enchantment in the world around us.

Nysien

The brother of Efnysien, and half-brother to Brân, Branwen, and Manawydan. Nysien and Efnysien comprise a pairing which reflects peace and conflict. Where Efnysien is said to be one who appears to feed on creating conflict, Nysien on the other hand is a weaver of peace. He has the ability to make peace between two groups in conflict, no matter how enraged they may be.

Nysien represents the lighter half of the brothers, he who facilitates peace and goodwill over conflict and anger. As a spiritual ally Nysien begs us to make peace, to seek resolution to conflicts as opposed to allowing conflicts to consume us.

Olwen

She of the white track. Olwen appears in the enigmatic tale of *How Culhwch won Olwen,* one of the oldest prose tales in Welsh tradition. She is daughter of Ysbaddaden Bencawr, a great giant. When a brave young man named Culhwch asks Ysbaddaden for Olwen's hand in marriage, the giant sends Culhwch on a series of seemingly impossible to accomplish quests. Eventually, however, with the help of Culhwch's cousin King Arthur and his men, they accomplish all the tasks and he is able to marry Olwen.

Olwen is an intriguing character. She dresses flamboyantly, adorned in scarlet silks, a red-gold torque around her neck, and dripping in exquisite jewellery featuring precious pearls and red stones. So opulent is she that when she takes her rings off to wash her hands, she cares not to put them back on, replacing them instead. Her hair is yellower than the flowers of the broom, her breasts paler than the breast of an elegant swan, and her cheeks are compared to the colour of the most vivid foxglove.

Her otherworldly beauty is matched by her magical nature. For wherever Olwen steps four white clovers spring up from the ground. Her very footsteps quicken and bring life to the soil, and this is why she is named Olwen, meaning 'white footprint' or 'white tracks'.

In the Welsh language many colloquial terms for aspects of the natural world carry Olwen's name. For example, white or Dutch clovers are sometimes referred to as M*eillion Olwen* (Olwen's clovers), great bindweed is referred to as *Moled Olwen* (Olwen's wimple) and even the milky way is sometimes referred to as *Llwybr Olwen* (Olwen's path).

The ethereal qualities surrounding Olwen seem to imply she is something fabulous and mystical in nature, such as a Goddess.

In modern polytheistic traditions Olwen is often revered as a Venusian Goddess – one who rules over love, beauty, and sensuality. She is also viewed as a solar Goddess due to her name being similar to the word for wheel in Welsh – Olwyn.

Penarddun

A somewhat shadowy figure, only truly mentioned in relation to other characters. She is the consort of Llŷr, and the mother of Llŷr's children Brân, Branwen, and Manawydan. She is also the mother of Efnisien and Nisien via a previous marriage to a man named Euroswydd. In the second branch of the *Mabinogi*, she is referred to as the daughter of Beli Mawr, though Rachel Bromwich in *Trioedd Ynys Prydein* notes that this might be an error, and that it is more likely Penarddun is the sister of Beli, rather than his daughter (Bromwich, 2014).

Penarddun's name can be split into two words: "Pen" meaning head or chief, and "Arddun" meaning beautiful, sublime, magnificent, or even dignified. Her name could also hold solar or light-based associations, and we might interpret her name as meaning the "radiant, beautiful head/chief".

Within a modern polytheistic context Penarddun is interpreted as the bridging force between the two dynastic families of Llŷr and Beli. Llŷr's house is usually associated with the realm of sea, and Beli's with the realm of sky, and so in this context she could also be viewed as the bridging force between sea and sky, light and water. If we ponder this on a more metaphorical level, she could be viewed as the uniting force between thought (sky/air) and emotion (sea/water). Because of these associations she is also associated with the physical manifestations of the combination of water and light. Rainbows, or the vision of a glorious sunset on a warm summer evening are how some might envision the magic of Penarddun.

Pryderi

The son of Rhiannon and Pwyll, Pryderi vanished on the night of his birth and his mother, Rhiannon, was accused of not only killing him, but cannibalising him. We discover later that some Otherworldly force had snatched Pryderi away and he had ended up in the home of a couple who had no children of their own. They raised him under the name Gwri wallt Euryn (Gwri of the golden hair). Eventually the couple realise who he is and return him to Rhiannon and Pwyll, and when they do Rhiannon utters that with his reappearance there can be an end to her anxiety. The word for 'anxiety' in Welsh is *pryder* and so he was named Pryderi.

Pryderi is the only character who is named and appears in all four branches of the *Mabinogi*. He is born in the first, he is a survivor of the great war in the second, he marries and is imprisoned in the third branch, and the fourth branch details his death.

Due to his appearance in all four branches some have speculated that the four branches of the *Mabinogi* were initially all focused on the story of Pryderi, the noble son (Stephens, 1986). All four branches do follow a timeline of his birth through to the inheritance of his land, and then finally to his death at the hands of Gwydion.

Pryderi is mentioned in the triads as one of the "Three Powerful Swineherds of the Island of Britain" (Bromwich, 2014). His role as a powerful swineherd is a reference to the fact that Arawn, the King of Annwfn, gifted his father Pwyll with fabulous Otherworldly creatures – pigs. Pigs were considered magical beings gifted to mortals by the chiefs of the Otherworld, and as such were incredibly sought after. In the fourth branch of the

Mabinogi Gwydion manipulates an entire war which he convinces his uncle, Math, is about the pigs in Pryderi's ownership.

He is described as the most gallant and handsome of men, skilled in anything he pursues. His valour is so great that only the trickery of Gwydion's magic is able to defeat him. He is eventually killed and buried atop Maentwrog above Y Felenrhyd, North Wales.

Like his father, Pryderi's name expresses an element of the human condition. The word *pryder* can be translated to mean either anxiety, care, or even loss. Throughout his escapades one could interpret his actions as being driven by the influence of anxieties. Anxiety often leads us to act in unwise ways, and Pryderi's challenge was to find his wisdom and act from a place of thought and caution as opposed to anxiety and fear. Pryderi reminds us to try and tame our anxieties, to not act on them alone, nor to allow the narratives our anxieties spin to rule our lives. Easier said than done, I know.

Pwyll

Prince of Dyfed, a Kingdom in the South of Wales, and consort of Rhiannon in the first branch of the *Mabinogi*. Pwyll is Pryderi's father. His name literally translates to mean caution, wisdom, and 'common sense', which is rather humorous when one considers he often acts without these qualities.

The first branch of the *Mabinogi* could be perceived as the story of Pwyll's ascendence from rash and thoughtlessness to becoming a wise, competent leader. This transformation occurs via his various interactions with the Otherworld. At the start of the first branch, he offends the King of Annwfn, Arawn, and he rectifies the situation by aiding Arawn in vanquishing his enemy, Hafgan. Arawn and Pwyll become friends, and a relationship blossoms between Annwfn and Dyfed. Later, Pwyll marries Rhiannon, an Otherworldly maiden, and when he acts thoughtlessly Rhiannon often cleans up his mess.

Rhiannon grants Pwyll the 'right to rule', acting as a sovereignty figure marrying the King/lord to his land. This union culminates in the birth of Pryderi, their son, the expansion of their territory, and the adoration of his people.

Pwyll, like his son Pryderi, as a spiritual or magical ally enables us to reflect on our very human qualities. The conditions which we must grapple with during our mortal existence. Pwyll reminds us to try and act with caution, patience, and wisdom throughout our lives. However, he also reminds us that there is always time to grow and change, for he often acted against the meaning of his name and yet he learnt from his past mistakes and grew into a wise, sage leader of his people.

Rhiannon

Rhiannon's name can be interpreted as meaning 'Great Queen' or 'Great Parent' (Davies, 2007). Originally betrothed to a man named Gwawl ap Clud, Rhiannon, unhappy with this match, ventures to Dyfed in order to catch the eye of the Lord of Dyfed, Pwyll. Her arrival is framed with magical themes. Pwyll stands atop a mound which local folklore states that those who look out from it shall either be mortally wounded or shall see something enchanting, a marvel.

Luckily for Pwyll it was the latter that came to pass. The enchanting thing he witnessed was Rhiannon. She rode across the scene upon the back of a great horse. She was dressed in golden brocaded silks, a fabric associated with the denizens of Annwfn, the Otherworld. Pwyll sent his men after her but no matter how quickly they rode their horses towards her they could never catch up, despite the fact she looked as though she was trotting at a leisurely pace. Eventually Pwyll chases her down himself and calls to her "for the love of the man you love the most, wait for me!". As he says these words Rhiannon stops, turns, and cheekily responds to him by saying "for the sake of your horse you should have asked me that sooner".

There is a layer of mysticism wrapped around this interaction. Pwyll initially sends his men galloping on horseback to pursue this mysterious, beautiful woman. However, no one can reach her unless she consents to allowing them to approach. Pwyll need only to have asked all along.

Throughout the *Mabinogi* Rhiannon expresses an aura of magic which further solidifies the notion that she is of Otherworldly origin. In the first branch she endures horrid slanders against her character, being accused of killing her own son, and yet she remains composed throughout such an ordeal. Eventually her son is returned to her, and when he is she says "Byddai gwared a'm pryder!" (begone my anxiety!). The word for anxiety here is *pryder* and in exclaiming this phrase whilst embracing her child she names him: Pryderi.

In the third branch of the *Mabinogi*, long after Pwyll, her original consort, has passed away she marries Manawydan fab Llŷr.

Rhiannon has various equine connections. In her very first appearance she is seen riding upon a tall, pale-white horse. When she gives birth to her son, and when her son is ultimately spirited away, this is mirrored by a nearby mare who gives birth to a foal which is also snatched away by some Otherworldly force. Later, in the third branch she is imprisoned in the Otherworld alongside her son Pryderi, and their imprisonment involves Rhiannon having collars usually worn by asses around her neck. These equine qualities have led some to associate Rhiannon as a Goddess of horses.

Though Rhiannon does not appear in the second branch of the *Mabinogi*, there is reference in this branch to the "Birds of Rhiannon". Mystical birds which have the ability to send all those who listen to their song into a liminal state of bliss. They are also mentioned in *Culhwch and Olwen* and described as birds capable of waking the dead and lulling the living into a sleep-like state. They soothe grief, grant a sense of serenity to the tortured and traumatised.

Rhiannon is a Goddess of Sovereignty. She grants would-be rulers the right to rule, representing the relationship between a lord and his land. She is associated with horses, grief, and there are parallels between her role in Welsh mythology to the stories of fairy brides in later folklore. Rhiannon is an Otherworldly maiden, and this along with the similarities between her and other fairy maidens have led many to dub her as a 'Queen of fairies'. She also represents the very spirit of the endurance of our people and our culture in Wales.

Taliesin

The most divinely inspired bard and prophet in all of time. Chief of all poets. Taliesin's name translates to mean 'the radiant brow'. References to Taliesin within written record extend as far back as the 9th century, though in the oldest references he is spoken of as though he is an established and well-known figure.

Best known today for the story of his birth, *Ystoria Taliesin,* which explores how Cerridwen, the Witch Goddess, wished to brew a potion of pure, distilled Awen that her son could drink. This potion, Cerridwen believed, could grant her son divine wisdom and great bardic skills. She longed for him to have such virtues due to the fact he was born tremendously ugly. Alas, the potion was ultimately drunk by another boy, Gwion Bach, whom Cerridwen pursued and swallowed in the form of a grain of wheat. Via the strangeness of magic, the grain transformed into a baby growing in Cerridwen's body, and once born he was set into the Otherworldly waters. Eventually he was fished out of the waters and named Taliesin. He grew to become the most profound of poets, a skilled prophet, a magician, and an icon of the bardic arts.

A medieval manuscript containing over sixty poems in middle Welsh is titled *The Book of Taliesin,* held in the National Library of Wales. The poems are attributed to Taliesin himself and include praise poems for Kings of the past, riddles, brain teasers, and poetry which delves into the mystical nature of life.

Taliesin is revered today as a chief of all poets, an inspiring force and the patron of all poets, storytellers, and artists. He is the archetypal knower, a being who drew his wisdom from the cauldron of Cerridwen and gifted the world with his insight. He sings the songs of creation, radiates the Awen, and grants us a glimpse into the truth of all things.

Ysbaddaden Bencawr

A giant, from the tale of *How Culhwch won Olwen*. His name translates to mean Hawthorn Chief Giant. The hero Culhwch wishes to marry Ysbaddaden's daughter, Olwen, and so seeks out the giant's permission. Culhwch is initially warned not to attempt winning Olwen's hand, as no man who has ever sought her hand in marriage has ever left Ysbaddaden's court alive. When Culhwch and his men do approach Ysbaddaden to ask his permission, the giant hurls spears with poisoned, iron tips at them. Fortunately, they catch the spears and throw them back towards Ysbaddaden – the spears pierce him in three parts of his body, his knee, chest, and eyeball.

Ysbaddaden is incredibly fearsome and large. His eyelids are so heavy that his servants must prop them up with large forks so that he may see what is before him. His hair is coarse and covers almost every part of his body. Eventually he sets Culhwch a series of seemingly endless and impossible tasks to complete in order to gain his permission to marry his daughter. These tasks include finding certain figures with specific skills, such as Amaethon, son of Dôn, Gwyn ap Nudd, and Mabon ap Modron. They also include incredibly difficult feats such as obtaining the blood of the very black witch, daughter of the very white witch, or obtaining a set of shears and a comb which rest behind the ears of a mystical boar named the Twrch Trwyth.

Culhwch sets out on these quests with King Arthur and his men. Eventually, with some difficulty, the tasks are completed one by one. They return to Ysbaddaden's court, groom the giant, and then ultimately Culhwch is granted permission to marry Olwen. Alas, this spells out death for the giant, for it is fated that once Ysbaddaden's daughter marries he will die. Culhwch's men kill Ysbaddaden, behead him, and stick his head on a spike.

Y Ddraig Goch

The mighty red dragon of Wales, who can be seen on our flag. Whilst it may seem strange to see the dragon on this list, as it may not seem like a typical Deity, the dragon has become emblematic of the very sovereignty and resilience of the Welsh.

The dragon has its roots in our myth and legend. The story of *Lludd and Llefelys* references two dragons battling every May Eve. One dragon is native, but the other is an invading dragon from another land. The screeching and tempestuous screaming echoing across the landscape by the battling dragons caused all the pregnant women in the land to miscarry. The terrifying screeching and the devastation such a sound causes is one of the three plagues the King of Britain, Lludd, has to face in the story. He is guided to a solution by his brother Llefelys, who instructs him to dig a hole at the very centre of Britain, place mead in the hole, as well as a sheet of brocaded silk. After he does this, he witnesses the dragons fighting and eventually, when they are exhausted, they plummet to the ground and fall directly into the hole, and onto the sheet of silk. As they hit the sheet, they transform into two little pigs. The pigs are so greedy that they cannot help but drink all the mead and fall so drunk that they drift off to sleep. Once they are asleep Lludd must wrap them up in the sheet tightly and bury them in a stone chest in the strongest place he can think of, which just so happens to be Dinas Emrys.

In the 9th century text the *Historia Brittonum,* we receive a story about a King who wants to build a castle in what is now Dinas Emrys. The castle walls fall down each night, and eventually a young Emrys (Merlin) enlightens the King that the reason this keeps occurring is because two dragons are battling beneath the Earth.

Both of these stories express the core legend of the dragon. The red dragon and the white dragon represent two opposing forces. The red represents the native Britons, or the Welsh, whilst the white dragon represents the invading forces. The white dragon appears large, strong, and fierce, whereas the red dragon appears to be timid and weak initially. As they fight, the white dragon seems to win, but at the very last moment every time, the red dragon rises and dominates the white, keeping it at bay. This is a prophecy for the native culture and people of Britain. A message that though we may seem defeated, our culture, language, and people will persist and rise over and over again.

The dragon represents our resilience in the face of hardship. Though the red dragon on our flag appears mighty and fierce, the dragon in the story is said to look timid in comparison to the fearsome white dragon. With that in mind, the dragon reminds us that though we may be small, we are mighty. Whatever is thrown our way, we will survive.

The red dragon represents our heart and spirit. It is the serpentine, telluric forces of our landscape. It is our fighting spirit, the fire within our bellies which burn passionately for this land of song and hope.

Chapter 9

Spirits Seen and Unseen

Beyond the Deities that sing the songs of our landscape, our culture, and our mythos, there have also always been a belief in beings which exist betwixt and between the mortal and divine. Beings that are difficult to fully categorise or understand. To us in the modern day, we might categorise these beings as "fairies". Though, it is important to note that the term "fairies" is an umbrella term under which many varied beings exist.

In Welsh culture and tradition, we have numerous native names for these liminal beings. In this section we will explore some beings which may play a role in the practice of a modern-day Polytheist, Pagan, or magical practitioner.

Y Tylwyth Teg – the Fair Family

Among modern Welsh language speakers, the term most used today to describe fairies is "Y Tylwyth Teg". This is an interesting term in and of itself, for it paints a picture of exactly who and what these beings are.

Y Tylwyth Teg translates to essentially mean "The Fair Family". To break it down: "Y" is simply Welsh for "the", whereas "Tylwyth" is a word which describes a family, genus, host, or grouping of related beings. Modern day speakers of Welsh might recognise the word Tylwyth as sounding similar to the word "Teulu" which translates to mean "family". This is because they share an etymological root. The final word "Teg" simply means fair, beautiful, or pleasant. Therefore "Y Tylwyth Teg" gives us a term which is used to define a grouping, family, or host of related beings which are described as being fair, or pleasant.

Whilst this might lead us to believe that the fair family are all incredibly pleasant beings, folklore would tell us otherwise. There are countless folk stories which detail ways the fair family would punish, curse, harm, or even torment mortals. Within lore surrounding folk magic we also know that mortals would craft charms and magical items in order to ward fairies away and would consult with magical specialists to help them keep the influence of fairies at bay. This begs the question, if fairies were known to cause mischief and harm to mortals, why would we call them "the fair family"?

The likelihood is that terms such as "Y Tylwyth Teg" were more protective euphemisms than descriptive names. It was commonly believed that fairies had the ability to travel invisibly, disguise themselves as ordinary mortals, and could hear all things said upon the winds. If people truly had a fear of these powerful, unpredictable, magical beings then I am certain they would do all in their power to avoid offending them, including speaking kindly of them at all times.

The majority of people wanted nothing to do with fairies. They would ward them away by hanging iron by the entryways to their doors, or by using plants and trees that they were said to be averse to, such as Gorse and Rowan.

However, if they did find themselves in a spot of bother with the fair folk, their first step to dealing with it was to visit their local magical specialist. Whilst the majority of the ordinary people within communities wanted nothing to do with fairies, for magical practitioners having a knowledge of, and even sometimes a relationship with the fairies was important to their work. Some magical practitioners claimed to learn much of their craft from the fairies, and that they walked hand in hand with them on special occasions throughout the year (Suggett, 2018). Fairies seemed to be part and package of the folk magical traditions of Wales,

Y Tylwyth Teg, the fair family, were denizens of the Otherworld. They visited our world from their own. As such, they are related with many Deities we find in Welsh lore. Whilst the term 'Y Tylwyth Teg' is never used within the context of our myths, such as the four branches of the *Mabinogi*, certain motifs and hints woven into the stories link certain beings to the fairies we see in later folklore. Arawn, for example, is a King of Annwfn, and the story of his interaction with Pwyll is similar to many other stories of mortals who come into contact with fairies and even spend extended periods of time living in the Otherworld, just like Pwyll.

The way we are introduced to Rhiannon in the first branch of the *Mabinogi* also echoes the stories we see in later folklore relating to fairy brides. In such stories, fairy maidens rise from deep lakes and marry mortal men. Rhiannon is, after all, an Otherworldly maiden who marries a mortal man. Perhaps her story is the prototypic version of the fairy bride legends found across Wales.

Llwyd ap Cilcoed is an Otherworldly man in the third branch who causes all manners of chaos and mischief in the lives of Manawydan, Pryderi, Rhiannon, and Cigfa. The way in which he torments the characters of that branch is comparable to the many stories we have of fairies playing tricks and taking revenge on mortals who they believe have wronged them in some manner.

The fairy beliefs and traditions of Wales, in my opinion, are deeply linked with the stories we find in our earliest myths. Folklore carries an echo of these tales which recount the link between fairies and mortals, our world and the Otherworld. I would recommend any Polytheist, Pagan, or magical practitioner find themselves a compendium of folk tales to acquaint themselves with our fairy traditions. Some suggested books would be W. Jenkyn Thomas' *The Welsh Fairy Book*, or Elias Owen's *Welsh Folk-Lore*. You could also find my book

Welsh Fairies if you have an interest in the relationship between magical practitioners and fairies, or have a desire to delve into fairy lore at a greater depth.

Bwbachod – Household Fairies

Whilst most people wanted nothing to do with fairies for the most part, there is one variety of fairy they could not ignore. That, of course, is the fairy of the household. Within Welsh tradition our household fairies are usually referred to as *Bwbachod* (plural) *Bwbach* (singular).

People would often leave offerings for the Bwbach of their house in the form of butter, milk, baked goods, or even occasionally alcohol. This was in part to establish good relationship with an entity you would be living in community with, but also occasionally with hopes of receiving something in return. There is evidence to suggest that some believed that if they kept the house clean, tidy, and warm, and left offerings out to the Bwbach, then they might leave gifts, or even churn your butter for you (Sikes, 1880).

Exercise: A Space for the Household Fairy

Clear a space in the home to act as a small altar for the household fairy. This space does not need to be large; a small table or shelf will suffice. Or perhaps even a corner of a countertop in the kitchen. Consider carefully where to set up this space, for it needs to be somewhere you pass often. Not a far away corner of the house you barely interact with.

The Bwbach is the spirit of the home, and as such they are felt most prominently in the very heart of the home. In times of old the heart of the house was the hearth. It was where the food was cooked, and where the family gathered to keep warm. Where is this in your home? It might be in the kitchen, where you host family meals. Or perhaps it is in the living room where you gather together to watch television and swap stories about your day. Think on this carefully, and choose your space wisely.

Once you have chosen the space, adorn it as you wish, with the Bwbach in mind. In my space I have a small brass ornament of a fairy creature, a bowl and cup to place offerings in, and a small metal dish I burn incense in. It is as simple as that. However, you can make it as elaborate or simple as you wish.

Come to this space as often as you are able. Keep it clean, light a candle for the household fairy, leave offerings, and see it as the bridge between you and the unseen dwellers of your home.

Ellyllon

As well as the Otherworldly denizens who visit our world, our folk tales and legends are also filled with strange, liminal entities who dwell in the wild places of our landscape. The common name we see associated with these beings is *Ellyllon* (plural). The Ellyllon are usually portrayed as small, goblin or elf-like beings who can be found in bogs, forests, ancient monuments, and haunting the ruins of abandoned places. They are often quite mischievous and troublesome, leading people who are wandering in the night astray and into danger.

Similar entities to the Ellyllon include the *Pwca,* shapeshifting troublemakers who love to torment Christians, and the *Coblynnau,* spirits of the mines, also known as knockers. These are phantom entities who haunt our land. Deeply connected with the natural world, yet ruled over still by Gwyn ap Nudd. When we work our magic out in the wild places, it is important to give a nod to these entities by leaving offerings for them, and attempting to avoid offending them by mistreating the landscape which is their home.

Conclusion

The Welsh Pantheon is one that is not restricted by antiquity alone. Our Gods carry an echo of beliefs, practices, and stories of a past now long forgotten. An echo of an oral tradition of storytelling which predates the coming of Christianity to these shores. They remind us of a time when our language, culture, and people were not pushed to the furthest corners of the landscape. A time when we had a greater sense of our own sovereignty. They carry with them the traumas and pains we have endured as a nation, and yet also remind us *Ry'n Ni Yma o Hyd!* We are still here. Despite everything that time has thrown at us, our culture and language persist. Our Gods carry that truth and embody them within their stories. They are part of the great tapestry that has led us to where we are today. Beyond all this, our Gods are now rooted in who we are as a modern nation, a modern people. Their stories continue to inspire us and propel us forward.

There is a larger corpus of myth, lore, and magic to draw upon than might first meet the eye. Though building a relationship with these Gods may sometimes feel like attempting to put together a jigsaw puzzle that is missing multiple pieces, as opposed to following a simple set of instructions, the outcome is always worth it. By connecting to the stream of Awen, and deciphering the complex song of our landscape, we gain stronger ties and connections to who we are.

How we move forward is completely up to us. There is a beauty to the freedom that exists in how we choose to interact with this material, and with the Gods who underly it all. We are a culture of song, of poetry, of resilience, and of magic. The Gods and spirits of this land remind us to take agency over our own lives, our own path.

In this book we have explored this topic in the broadest and simplest of ways. My hope is that you, as the reader, now take what you have learnt here and apply it to your own practice. Dig deeper, seek out further knowledge. After all, research and study can be a powerful and transformative devotional act. Find community, whether that be in person or online, to share your thoughts, insights, and wisdom with.

The world around us is alive. We live in constant community with neighbours that are both seen and unseen. And yet, even those who remain unseen are felt. Seek the magic in the everyday, and in the landscape around you. For it is there you will hear the sweet song of the Birds of Rhiannon. That is where the winds will carry whispers of arcane, hidden knowledge to your ears, just as it did for Math. It is in these wild places we will catch glimpses of the Tylwyth Teg dancing, and spectral hounds running through the bracken. Be like Brân, and become a bridge between the mundane and the magical. Re-enchant the world with the wisdom that can be found right at our fingertips.

A Guide to Welsh Pronunciation

For those who have no experience with hearing the Welsh language being spoken, the names, place names, and certain words mentioned throughout this book may seem daunting. How does one pronounce *Pwyll* or *Manawydan*? Whilst the Welsh language may seem daunting, fear not! The rules of pronunciation are fairly simple, and once you know said rules, you will be able to learn to read Welsh words with ease.

Welsh is a phonetic language, and therefore once you learn how to pronounce each letter in the alphabet, it is fairly easy to deduce how a word should sound. In the English language one singular letter may be pronounced several different ways. For example, the word *Aggravating* in English has three a's, and the sound the a makes is different on all three occasions. The first is an 'ah' sound, the second an 'uh' sound, and the third an 'ay' sound.

This is incredibly rare in the Welsh language, Once you have discovered the sound a letter makes, it is likely that letter will always sound that way. For example, A in the Welsh alphabet is pronounced 'Ah'. So, whether you see an A in words such as *Afal* (apple), *Aros* (wait), or *Annwfn* (The Otherworld) that 'A' in all these words is pronounced 'Ah'.

Keeping this in mind, one of the easiest methods of learning how to pronounce words in Welsh relatively quickly, is to familiarise yourself with the Welsh alphabet.

The Welsh Alphabet

a, b, c, ch, d, dd, e, f, ff, g, ng, h, i, l, ll, m, n, o, p, ph, r, rh, s, t, th, u, w, y

As I have mentioned, it is very rarely that a word will change its pronunciation in Welsh, especially when compared to English.

This makes learning pronunciations easier. However, I keep stating that it is 'rare' a letter will change its sound, and that implies there are certain situations where the sound will indeed change, so what are these situations?

The letter 'Y'

The letter Y appears frequently in Welsh words, as it is a vowel in our language. Even in the Welsh version of the term *'The Mabinogi'*, you will see that it becomes *'Y Mabinogi'*. In this context the letter Y is actually a full word! It translates to mean 'the'. In *'Y Mabinogi'* the Y is pronounced 'uh', similar to how the letter U sounds in English words such as sun, fun, or turn.

However, the letter Y is a complicated letter in Welsh, as it is the only letter which really changes its sound depending on context. For example, the word *Ysbyty* (hospital) has three Y's, the first two Y's are pronounced as I explained above, with an 'uh' sound. The third 'Y', however, is pronounced a tad differently. There is no English equivalent to explain how it is pronounced here, the closest is that it sounds similar to the sound a double E makes in words such as bee, or tree.

The Y only changes to make the 'ee' sound in certain words, predominantly multi-syllabic words with multiple Y's, and also when a circumflex can be found above the Y as such: ŷ.

The Circumflex, or 'Little Roof'

Another occasion where letters will change in their pronunciation is when a circumflex is present. In Welsh we refer to the circumflex as a *'To Bach'* which translates literally to mean a 'little roof'. Because that is exactly what it looks like, a little roof above the letters. You will find a circumflex above vowels in certain words.

A rather tired and uneducated joke about the Welsh language is that we supposedly have no vowels. This isn't true, the reason

English speakers may believe this is because we have a different set of vowels to the English language. Our vowels are as follows:

a, e, i, o, u, w, y

Technically, we have more vowels than English! And each vowel is pronounced as such:

A = 'ah', as in 'Apple'.
E = as in the 'e' in 'bed', never as in 'be'.
I = 'ee', as in the double ee in 'tree'.
O = 'Aw', as in the 'O' in 'from'.
U = A slightly difficult one for non-Welsh speakers. Essentially an 'ee' noise, as in 'tree', but with the tongue rolled into the shape of a 'U'.
W – 'ooh', as in the noise the double o makes in 'food'.
Y – As mentioned earlier, this is one of the only Welsh letters which can change depending on context. For the most part 'Y' is pronounced 'Uh', as in the sound U makes in English in words such as 'turn', or like the noise e makes in words such as 'The'. However, sometimes, usually in multi-syllabic words, the Y becomes more of an 'ee' sound, more or less indistinguishable from the Welsh 'U'. The best word to showcase this difference in pronunciation is 'Ysbyty', the Welsh word for 'hospital', which has three Y's. The first two Y's are pronounced as 'Uh', whereas the final Y is pronounced more so as an ee noise. Uss-BUTT-ee.

When the vowels have a circumflex above them, they will look like this:

â, ê, î, ô, û, ŵ, ŷ

The purpose of the circumflex is to extend the sound of the letter. So, for example, an A goes from being an 'ah' to a longer, more pronounced 'aah'. This is a difficult concept to explain in writing, and therefore I suggest looking to my YouTube videos for further clarity.

Over on my YouTube channel I already have several videos which go through the pronunciation of names, and words featured in Welsh myth and lore. You can find me under the username *'Mhara Starling'*.

Double Letters

Another fairly daunting aspect of the Welsh language may be the appearance of seemingly 'double letter' letters in our alphabet. These are as follows:

ch, dd, ff, ng, ll, ph, rh, and th

To those whose first language is English, it may seem strange to consider what appears to be two letters together as one singular letter. However, individual letters they are. Each of these letters create a specific sound as follows:

ch – a throaty sound, emanating from the back of the throat. Similar to how a Scottish person would pronounce the ch in loch. It is not an S sound, nor a sound similar to the ch in English words such as cheek.

dd – The sound of this letter comes from the front of the mouth. Similar to the sound of th in English words such as there, them and this but not like the th sound in English words such as thick or thin.

ff – This is a hard F sound as in the English words fight, freedom or full. The singular f in Welsh is a V noise as in video.

ng – Thing of ng as the same sound found at the end of English words such as thinking, listening, or singing.
ll – The double L letter is one of the most complex Welsh letters. There is no English counterpart. It is a sound similar to that of a hiss.
ph – Simply pronounced similarly to the ph in the English word phrase.
rh – Very similar to a rolling R sound when used within words. Roll your R and then exhale or sigh while doing so.
th – Pronounced as the th in the English words thick, and thin.

For more help with pronunciation, find my channel on YouTube where I have uploaded a variety of videos breaking down the pronunciation of Welsh words, and in particular the names of Deities. You can find my channel by searching for *'Mhara Starling'*.

Bibliography

ab Ithel, J. W. (2004). *Barddas; Or, a Collection of Original Documents, Illustrative of the Theology, Wisdom, and Usages of the Bardo-druidic System of the Isle of Britain.* Red Wheel/Weiser.

Bromwich, R. (Ed.). (2014). *Trioedd Ynys Prydein: The Triads of the Island of Britain.* University of Wales Press.

Charles-Edwards, T. M. (2020). *The Date of the Four Branches of the Mabinogi.* In *The Mabinogi (Routledge Revivals),* (pp. 19-58). Routledge.

Conran, T. (2017). *Welsh Verse: Fourteen Centuries of Poetry.* Poetry Wales Press Ltd., Bridgend.

Davies, J. (1999). *A Pocket Guide: The Welsh Language.* University of Wales Press.

Davies, S. (1989). *Pedeir Keinc y Mabinogi.* Gomer Press.

Davies, S. (1993). *The Four Branches of the Mabinogi: Pedeir Keinc y Mabinogi.* Gomer Press, Llandysul.

Davies, Sioned. (2007). *The Mabinogion.* Oxford University Press, USA.

Green, M and Howell, R. (2000). *A Pocket Guide: Celtic Wales,* University of Wales Press.

Hansen, W. (2004). *Classical Mythology: A Guide to the Mythical World of the Greeks and Romans,* Oxford University Press, New York, NY.

Haycock, M. (2007). *Legendary poems from the Book of Taliesin.* CMCS publications.

Hughes, K. (2014). *The Book of Celtic Magic: Transformative Teachings from the Cauldron of Awen.* Llewellyn Worldwide, Woodbury, MN.

Hughes, K. (2021). *Cerridwen: Celtic Goddess of Inspiration.* Llewellyn Worldwide, Woodbury, MN.

Ifans, D. & Ifans, R. (2007) *Y Mabinogion.* Wasg Gomer, Ceredigion.

Jones, T.G. (1930). *Welsh Folklore and Folk Custom.* Cockatrice Books. Facsimile Edition (2020).

Lindahl, C, McNamara, J, and Lindow, J. (Eds.) (2002). *Medieval Folklore: A Guide to Myths, Legends, Tales, Beliefs, and Customs.* Oxford University Press, New York.

Morus-Bairs, G. (2023). *Taliesin Origins: Exploring the Myth of the Greatest Celtic Bard.* Celtic Source.

Owen, E. (1887). *Welsh Folk-Lore: A Collection of Folk-Tales and Legends of North Wales.* Facsimile Edition (1976). EP Publishing Limited, Wrexham.

Owen, T.M. (1959). *Welsh Folk Customs.* Gomerian Press, Llandysul.

Rodway, S. (2018). *The Mabinogi and the shadow of Celtic mythology.* Studia Celtica, 52(1), 67-85.

Ross, A. (2001). *Folklore of Wales.* The History Press, Stroud.

Rudiger, A. (2021). *Y Tylwyth Teg. an Analysis of a Literary Motif.* Bangor University (United Kingdom).

Sikes, W. (1880). *British Goblins: Welsh Folk-Lore, Fairy Mythology, Legends and Traditions.* Pranava Books, Facsimile Edition.

Starling, M. (2022). *Welsh Witchcraft: A Guide to the Spirits, Lore, and Magic of Wales.* Llewellyn Worldwide, Woodbury, MN.

Starling, M. (2024). *Welsh Fairies: A Guide to the Lore, Legends, Denizens & Deities of the Otherworld.* Llewellyn Worldwide, Woodbury, MN.

Stephens, M. (ed.). (1986). *The Oxford Companion to the Literature of Wales.* Oxford University Press, Oxford.

Suggett, R. (2018). *Welsh Witches: Narratives of Witchcraft and Magic from* 16th *and* 17th *Century Wales.* Atramentous Press.

Sullian III, C.W. (ed.). (1996). *The Mabinogi: A Book of Essays.* Garland Publishing, inc., Oxon.

Thomas, G. (1976). *Y Traddodiad Barddol.* Gwasg Prifysgol Cymru, Cardiff.

Thomas, W. J. (1907). *The Welsh Fairy Book.* TF Unwin. (Facsimile Copy).

Williams, M. (2019). *Magic and Marvels*. In Evans, G and Fulton, H. (Eds.). (2019). *The Cambridge History of Welsh Literature*. Cambridge University Press.

Williams, M. (2021). *The Celtic Myths That Shape the Way We Think*. Thames & Hudson, London.

Other Books in the *Pantheon* Series

The Egyptians
Robin Herne
978-1-78535-504-2 (Paperback)
978-1-78535-505-9 (e-book)

The Greeks
Irisanya Moon
978-1-78535-506-6 (Paperback)
978-1-78535-507-3 (e-book)

The Irish
Morgan Daimler
978-1-80341-649-6 (Paperback)
978-1-80341-648-9 (e-book)

The Norse
Morgan Daimler
978-1-78904-141-5 (Paperback)
978-1-78904-142-2 (e-book)

The Romans
Rachel Roberts
978-1-80341-682-3 (Paperback)
978-1-80341-930-5 (e-book)

The Minoans
Laura Perry
978-1-80341-627-4 (Paperback)
978-1-80341-914-5 (e-book)

MOON BOOKS

PAGANISM & SHAMANISM

What is Paganism? A religion, a spirituality, an alternative belief system, nature worship? You can find support for all these definitions (and many more) in dictionaries, encyclopaedias, and text books of religion, but subscribe to any one and the truth will evade you. Above all Paganism is a creative pursuit, an encounter with reality, an exploration of meaning and an expression of the soul. Druids, Heathens, Wiccans and others, all contribute their insights and literary riches to the Pagan tradition. Moon Books invites you to begin or to deepen your own encounter, right here, right now.

If you have enjoyed this book, why not tell other readers by posting a review on your preferred book site.

Bestsellers from Moon Books

Keeping Her Keys
An Introduction to Hekate's Modern Witchcraft
Cyndi Brannen
Blending Hekate, witchcraft and personal development together to create a powerful new magickal perspective.
Paperback: 978-1-78904-075-3 ebook 978-1-78904-076-0

Journey to the Dark Goddess
How to Return to Your Soul
Jane Meredith
Discover the powerful secrets of the Dark Goddess and transform your depression, grief and pain into healing and integration.
Paperback: 978-1-84694-677-6 ebook: 978-1-78099-223-5

Shamanic Reiki
Expanded Ways of Working with Universal Life Force Energy
Llyn Roberts, Robert Levy
Shamanism and Reiki are each powerful ways of healing; together, their power multiplies. Shamanic Reiki introduces techniques to help healers and Reiki practitioners tap ancient healing wisdom.
Paperback: 978-1-84694-037-8 ebook: 978-1-84694-650-9

Southern Cunning
Folkloric Witchcraft in the American South
Aaron Oberon
Modern witchcraft with a Southern flair, this book is a journey through the folklore of the American South and a look at the power these stories hold for modern witches.
Paperback: 978-1-78904-196-5 ebook: 978-1-78904-197-2

Bestsellers from Moon Books
Pagan Portals Series

The Morrigan

Meeting the Great Queens

Morgan Daimler

Ancient and enigmatic, the Morrigan reaches out to us. On shadowed wings and in raven's call, meet the ancient Irish goddess of war, battle, prophecy, death, sovereignty, and magic.

Paperback: 978-1-78279-833-0 ebook: 978-1-78279-834-7

The Awen Alone

Walking the Path of the Solitary Druid

Joanna van der Hoeven

An introductory guide for the solitary Druid, The Awen Alone will accompany you as you explore, and seek out your own place within the natural world.

Paperback: 978-1-78279-547-6 ebook: 978-1-78279-546-9

Moon Magic

Rachel Patterson

An introduction to working with the phases of the Moon, what they are and how to live in harmony with the lunar year and to utilise all the magical powers it provides.

Paperback: 978-1-78279-281-9 ebook: 978-1-78279-282-6

Hekate

A Devotional

Vivienne Moss

Hekate, Queen of Witches and the Shadow-Lands, haunts the pages of this devotional bringing magic and enchantment into your lives.

Paperback: 978-1-78535-161-7 ebook: 978-1-78535-162-4

Readers of ebooks can buy or view any of these bestsellers by clicking on the live link in the title. Most titles are published in paperback and as an ebook. Paperbacks are available in traditional bookshops. Both print and ebook formats are available online.

Find more titles and sign up to our readers' newsletter
www.collectiveinkbooks.com/paganism

For video content, author interviews and more, please subscribe to our YouTube channel.

MoonBooksPublishing

Follow us on social media for book news, promotions and more:

Facebook: Moon Books

Instagram: @MoonBooksCI

X: @MoonBooksCI

TikTok: @MoonBooksCI